YOUR PERSONAL
HOROSCOPE
2019

ARIES

GW00640812

YOUR PERSONAL
HOROSCOPE
2019

ARIES

21st March–20th April

igloobooks

igloobooks

Published in 2018
by Igloo Books Ltd
Cottage Farm
Sywell
NN6 0BJ
www.igloobooks.com

Copyright © 2018 Foulsham Publishing Ltd

Produced for Igloo Books by Foulsham Publishing Ltd, The Old Barrel Store,
Drayman's Lane, Marlow, Bucks SL7 2FF, England

The Copyright Act prohibits (subject to certain very limited exceptions) the making of copies of
any copyright work or of a substantial part of such a work, including the making of copies by
photocopying or similar process. Written permission to make a copy or copies must therefore
normally be obtained from the publisher in advance. It is advisable also to consult the publisher if
in any doubt as to the legality of any copying which is to be undertaken.

FIR003 0718
2 4 6 8 10 9 7 5 3 1
ISBN: 978-1-78810-498-2

This is an abridged version of material originally published
in Old Moore's Horoscope and Astral Diary.

Cover designed by Nicholas Gage
Edited by Bobby Newlyn-Jones

Printed and manufactured in China

CONTENTS

INTRODUCTION

Your personal horoscopes have been specifically created to allow you to get the most from astrological patterns and the way they have a bearing on not only your zodiac sign, but nuances within it. Using the diary section of the book you can read about the influences and possibilities of each and every day of the year. It will be possible for you to see when you are likely to be cheerful and happy or those times when your nature is in retreat and you will be more circumspect. The diary will help to give you a feel for the specific 'cycles' of astrology and the way they can subtly change your day-to-day life. For example, when you see the sign ☿, this means that the planet Mercury is retrograde at that time. Retrograde means it appears to be running backwards through the zodiac. Such a happening has a significant effect on communication skills, but this is only one small aspect of how the personal horoscope can help you.

With your personal horoscope the story doesn't end with the diary pages. It includes simple ways for you to work out the zodiac sign the Moon occupied at the time of your birth, and what this means for your personality. In addition, if you know the time of day you were born, it is possible to discover your Ascendant, yet another important guide to your personal make-up and potential.

Many readers are interested in relationships and in knowing how well they get on with people of other astrological signs. You might also be interested in the way you appear to very different sorts of individuals. If you are such a person, the section on Venus will be of particular interest. Despite the rapidly changing position of this planet, you can work out your Venus sign, and learn what bearing it will have on your life.

Using your personal horoscope you can travel on one of the most fascinating and rewarding journeys that anyone can take – the journey to a better realisation of self.

7

THE ESSENCE
OF ARIES

Exploring the Personality of Aries the Ram

(21ST MARCH – 20TH APRIL)

What's in a sign?

Aries is not the first sign of the zodiac by accident. It's the place in the year when the spring begins, and so it represents some of the most dynamic forces in nature, and within the zodiac as a whole. As a result the very essence of your nature is geared towards promoting yourself in life and pushing your ideas forward very positively. You don't brook a great deal of interference in your life, but you are quite willing to help others as much as you can, provided that to do so doesn't curb your natural desire to get on in life.

Aries people are not universally liked, though your true friends remain loyal to you under almost any circumstances. But why should it be that such a dynamic and go-getting person does meet with some opposition? The answer is simple: not everyone is quite so sure of themselves as you are and many tend to get nervous when faced with the sheer power of the Aries personality. If there is one factor within your own control that could counter these problems it is the adoption of some humility – that commodity which is so important for you to dredge from the depths of your nature. If you only show the world that you are human, and that you are well aware of the fact, most people would follow you willingly to the very gates of hell. The most successful Aries subjects know this fact and cultivate it to the full.

Your executive skills are never in doubt and you can get almost anything practical done whilst others are still jumping from foot to foot. That's why you are such a good organiser and are so likely to be out there at the front of any venture. Adventurous and quite willing to show your bravery in public, you can even surprise yourself sometimes with the limits you are likely to go to in order to reach solutions that seem right to you.

Kind to those you take to, you can be universally loved when working at your best. Despite this there will be times in your life when you simply can't understand why some people just don't like you. Maybe there's an element of jealousy involved.

Aries resources

The part of the zodiac occupied by the sign of Aries has, for many centuries, been recognised as the home of self-awareness. This means that there isn't a person anywhere else in the zodiac that has a better knowledge of self than you do. But this isn't necessarily an intellectual process with Aries, more a response to the very blood that is coursing through your veins. Aries' success doesn't so much come from spending hours working out the pros and cons of any given course of action, more from the thrill of actually getting stuck in. If you find yourself forced into a life that means constantly having to think everything through to the tiniest detail, there is likely to be some frustration in evidence.

Aries is ruled by Mars, arguably the most go-getting of all the planets in the solar system. Mars is martial and demands practical ways of expressing latent power. It also requires absolute obedience from subordinates. When this is forthcoming, Aries individuals are the most magnanimous people to be found anywhere. Loyalty is not a problem and there have been many instances in history when Aries people were quite willing to die for their friends if necessary.

When other people are willing to give up and go with the flow, you will still be out there pitching for the result that seems most advantageous to you. It isn't something you can particularly control and those who don't know you well could find you sometimes curt and over-demanding as a result. But because you are tenacious you can pick the bones out of any situation and will usually arrive at your desired destination, if you don't collapse with fatigue on the way.

Routines, or having to take life at the pace of less motivated types, won't suit you at all. Imprisonment of any sort, even in a failed relationship, is sheer torture and you will move heaven and earth to get out into the big, wide world, where you can exploit your natural potential to the full. Few people know you really well because you don't always explain yourself adequately. The ones who do adore you.

Beneath the surface

Whereas some zodiac signs are likely to spend a great deal of their lives looking carefully at the innermost recesses of their own minds, Aries individuals tend to prefer the cut and thrust of the practical world. Aries people are not natural philosophers, but that doesn't mean that you aren't just as complicated beneath the surface as any of your astrological brothers and sisters. So what is it that makes the Aries firebrand think and act in the way that it does? To a great extent it is a lack of basic self-confidence.

This statement might seem rather odd, bearing in mind that a fair percentage of the people running our world were born under the sign of the Ram, but it is true nevertheless. Why? Because people who know themselves and their capabilities really well don't feel the constant need to prove themselves in the way that is the driving force of your zodiac sign. Not that your naturally progressive tendencies are a fault. On the contrary, if used correctly they can help you to create a better, fairer and happier world, at least in your own vicinity.

The fact that you occasionally take your ball and go home if you can't get your own way is really down to the same insecurity that is noticeable through many facets of your nature. If Aries can't rule, it often doesn't want to play at all. A deep resentment and a brooding quality can build up in the minds and souls of some thwarted Aries types, a tendency that you need to combat. Better by far to try and compromise, itself a word that doesn't exist in the vocabularies of the least enlightened people born under the sign of the Ram. Once this lesson is learned, inner happiness increases and you relax into your life much more.

The way you think about others is directly related to the way you consider they think about you. This leads to another surprising fact regarding the zodiac sign. Aries people absolutely hate to be disliked, though they would move heaven and earth to prove that this isn't the case. And as a result Aries both loves and hates with a passion. Deep inside you can sometimes be a child shivering in the dark. If you only realise this fact your path to happiness and success is almost assured. Of course to do so takes a good deal of courage – but that's a commodity you don't lack.

Making the best of yourself

It would be quite clear to any observer that you are not the sort of person who likes to hang around at the back of a queue, or who would relish constantly taking orders from people who may not know situations as well as you do. For that reason alone you are better in positions that see you out there at the front, giving commands and enjoying the cut and thrust of everyday life. In a career sense this means that whatever you do you are happiest telling those around you how to do it too. Many Aries people quite naturally find their way to the top of the tree and don't usually have too much trouble staying there.

It is important to remember, however, that there is another side to your nature: the giving qualities beneath your natural dominance. You can always be around when people need you the most, encouraging and even gently pushing when it is necessary. By keeping friends and being willing to nurture relationships across a broad spectrum, you gradually get to know what makes those around you tick. This makes for a more patient and understanding sort of Aries subject – the most potent of all.

Even your resilience is not endless, which is why it is important to remember that there are times when you need rest. Bearing in mind that you are not superhuman is the hardest lesson to learn, but the admission brings humility, something that Aries needs to cultivate whenever possible.

Try to avoid living a restricted life and make your social contacts frequent and important. Realise that there is much more to life than work and spend some of your free time genuinely attempting to help those who are less well off than you are. Crucially you must remember that 'help' is not the same as domination.

The impressions you give

This section may well be of less interest to Aries subjects than it would be to certain other zodiac signs. The reason is quite clear. Aries people are far less interested in what others think about them than almost anyone else – or at least they tell themselves that they are. Either way it is counterproductive to ignore the opinions of the world at large because to do so creates stumbling blocks, even in a practical sense.

Those around you probably find you extremely capable and well able to deal with almost any situation that comes your way. Most are willing to rely heavily on you and the majority would almost instinctively see you as a leader. Whether or not they like you at the same time is dependent on the way you handle situations. That's the difference between the go-getting, sometimes selfish type of Aries subject and the more enlightened amongst this illustrious sign.

You are viewed as being exciting and well able to raise enthusiasm for almost any project that takes your fancy. Of course this implies a great responsibility because you are always expected to come up with the goods. The world tends to put certain people on a pedestal, and you are one of them. On the other side of the coin we are all inclined to fire arrows at the elevated, so maintaining your position isn't very easy.

Most of the time you are seen as being magnanimous and kind, factors that you can exploit, whilst at the same time recognising the depth of the responsibility that comes with being an Aries subject. It might not be a bad thing to allow those around you to see that you too have feet of clay. This will make them respect and support you all the more, and even Aries people really do need to feel loved. A well-balanced Aries subject is one of the most elevated spirits to be found anywhere.

The way forward

You certainly enjoy life more when looking at it from the top of the tree. Struggling to get by is not in the least interesting to your zodiac sign and you can soon become miserable if things are not going well for you. That's why it is probably quite justified in your case to work tenaciously in order to achieve your objectives. Ideally, once you have realised some sort of success and security for yourself, you should then be willing to sit and watch life go by a little more. In fact this doesn't happen. The reason for this is clear. The Aries subject who learns how to succeed rarely knows when to stop – it's as simple as that.

Splitting your life into different components can help, if only because this means that you don't get the various elements mixed up. So, for example, don't confuse your love life with your professional needs, or your family with colleagues. This process allows you to view life in manageable chunks and also makes it possible for you to realise when any one of them may be working well. As a result you will put the effort where it's needed, and enjoy what is going well for you.

If you want to know real happiness you will also have to learn that acquisition for its own sake brings hollow rewards at best. When your talents are being turned outward to the world at large, you are one of the most potent and successful people around. What is more you should find yourself to be a much happier person when you are lending a hand to the wider world. This is possible, maybe outside of your normal professional sphere, though even where voluntary work is concerned it is important not to push yourself to the point of fatigue.

Keep yourself physically fit, without necessarily expecting that you can run to the South Pole and back, and stay away from too many stimulants, such as alcohol and nicotine. The fact is that you are best when living a healthy life, but it doesn't help either if you make even abstinence into an art form. Balance is important, as is moderation – itself a word that is difficult for you to understand. In terms of your approach to other people it's important to realise that everyone has a specific point of view. These might be different to yours, but they are not necessarily wrong. Sort out the friends who are most important to you and stick with them, whilst at the same time realising that almost everyone can be a pal – with just a little effort.

ARIES ON THE CUSP

Astrological profiles are altered for those people born at either the beginning or the end of a zodiac sign, or, more properly, on the cusps of a sign. In the case of Aries this would be on the 21st of March and for two or three days after, and similarly at the end of the sign, probably from the 18th to the 20th of April.

The Pisces Cusp – 21st March to 24th March

With the Sun so close to the zodiac sign of Pisces at the time you were born, it is distinctly possible that you have always had some doubts when reading a character breakdown written specifically for the sign of Aries. This isn't surprising because no zodiac sign has a definite start or end, they merely merge together. As a result there are some of the characteristics of the sign of the Fishes that are intermingled with the qualities of Aries in your nature.

What we probably find, as a result, is a greater degree of emotional sensitivity and a tendency to be more cognisant of what the rest of humanity is feeling. This is not to imply that Aries is unfeeling, but rather that Pisceans actively make humanity their business.

You are still able to achieve your most desired objectives in the practical world, but on the way, you stop to listen to the heartbeat of the planet on which you live. A very good thing, of course, but at the same time there is some conflict created if your slightly dream-like tendencies get in the way of your absolute need to see things through to their logical conclusion.

Nobody knows you better than you know yourself, or at least that's what the Aries qualities within you say, but that isn't always verified by some of the self-doubt that comes from the direction of the Fishes. As in all matters astrological, a position of balance has to be achieved in order to reconcile the differing qualities of your nature. In your case, this is best accomplished by being willing to stop and think once in a while and by refusing to allow your depth to be a problem.

Dealt with properly, the conjoining of Pisces and Aries can be a wondrous and joyful affair, a harmony of opposites that always makes you interesting to know. Your position in the world is naturally one of authority but at the same time you need to serve. That's why some people with this sort of mixture of astrological qualities would make such good administrators in a hospital, or in any position where the alternate astrological needs are well balanced. In the chocolate box of life you are certainly a 'soft centre'.

The Taurus Cusp – 18th April to 20th April

The merge from Aries to Taurus is much less well defined than the one at the other side of Aries, but it can be very useful to you all the same. Like the Pisces-influenced Aries you may be slightly more quiet than would be the case with the Ram taken alone and your thought processes are probably not quite as fast. But to compensate for this fact you don't rush into things quite as much and are willing to allow ideas to mature more fully.

Your sense of harmony and beauty is strong and you know, in a very definite way, exactly what you want. As a result your home will be distinctive but tasteful and it's a place where you need space to be alone sometimes, which the true Aries subject probably does not. You do not lack the confidence to make things look the way you want them, but you have a need to display these things to the world at large and sometimes even to talk about how good you are at decoration and design.

If anyone finds you pushy, it is probably because they don't really know what makes you tick. Although you are willing to mix with almost anyone, you are more inclined, at base, to have a few very close friends who stay at the forefront of your life for a long time. It is likely that you enjoy refined company and you wouldn't take kindly to the dark, the sordid, or the downright crude in life.

Things don't get you down as much as can sometimes be seen to be the case for Taurus when taken alone and you are rarely stumped for a progressive and practical idea when one is needed most. At all levels, your creative energy is evident and some of you even have the ability to make this into a business, since Aries offers the practical and administrative spark that Taurus can sometimes lack.

In matters of love, you are ardent and sincere, probably an idealist, and you know what you want in a partner. Whilst this is also true in the case of Taurus, you are different, because you are much more likely, not only to look, but also to say something about the way you feel.

Being naturally friendly you rarely go short of the right sort of help and support when it is most vital. Part of the reason for this lies in the fact that you are so willing to be the sounding-board for the concerns of your friends. All in all you can be very contented with your lot, but you never stop searching for something better all the same. At its best, this is one of the most progressive cuspal matches of them all.

ARIES AND ITS ASCENDANTS

The nature of every individual on the planet is composed of the rich variety of zodiac signs and planetary positions that were present at the time of their birth. Your Sun sign, which in your case is Aries, is one of the many factors when it comes to assessing the unique person you are. Probably the most important consideration, other than your Sun sign, is to establish the zodiac sign that was rising over the eastern horizon at the time that you were born. This is your Ascending or Rising sign. Most popular astrology fails to take account of the Ascendant, and yet its importance remains with you from the very moment of your birth, through every day of your life. The Ascendant is evident in the way you approach the world, and so, when meeting a person for the first time, it is this astrological influence that you are most likely to notice first. Our Ascending sign essentially represents what we appear to be, while our Sun sign is what we feel inside ourselves.

The Ascendant also has the potential for modifying our overall nature. For example, if you were born at a time of day when Aries was passing over the eastern horizon (this would be around the time of dawn) then you would be classed as a double Aries. As such you would typify this zodiac sign, both internally and in your dealings with others. However, if your Ascendant sign turned out to be a Water sign, such as Pisces, there would be a profound alteration of nature, away from the expected qualities of Aries.

One of the reasons that popular astrology often ignores the Ascendant is that it has always been rather difficult to establish. We have found a way to make this possible by devising an easy-to-use table, which you will find on page 157 of this book. Using this, you can establish your Ascendant sign at a glance. You will need to know your rough time of birth, then it is simply a case of following the instructions.

For those readers who have no idea of their time of birth it might be worth allowing a good friend, or perhaps your partner, to read through the section that follows this introduction. Someone who deals with you on a regular basis may easily discover your Ascending sign, even though you could have some difficulty establishing it for yourself. A good understanding of this component of your nature is essential if you want to be aware of that 'other person' who is responsible for the way you make contact with the world at large. Your Sun sign, Ascendant sign, and the other pointers in this book will, together, allow you a far better understanding of what makes you tick as an individual. Peeling back the different layers of your astrological make-up can be an enlightening experience, and the Ascendant may represent one of the most important layers of all.

Aries with Aries Ascendant

What you see is what you get with this combination. You typify the no-nonsense approach of Aries at its best. All the same this combination is quite daunting when viewed through the eyes of other, less dominant sorts of people. You tend to push your way though situations that would find others cowering in a corner and you are afraid of very little. With a determination to succeed that makes you a force to be reckoned with, you leave the world in no doubt as to your intentions and tend to be rather too brusque for your own good on occasions.

At heart you are kind and loving, able to offer assistance to the downtrodden and sad, and usually willing to take on board the cares of people who have a part to play in your life. No-one would doubt your sincerity, or your honesty, though you may utilise slightly less than orthodox ways of getting your own way on those occasions when you feel you have right on your side. You are a loving partner and a good parent, though where children are concerned you tend to be rather too protective. The trouble is that you know what a big, bad world it can be and probably feel that you are better equipped to deal with things than anyone else.

Aries with Taurus Ascendant

This is a much quieter combination, so much so that even experienced astrologers would be unlikely to recognise you as an Aries subject at all, unless of course they came to know you very well. Your approach to life tends to be quiet and considered and there is a great danger that you could suppress those feelings that others of your kind would be only too willing to verbalise. To compensate you are deeply creative and will think matters through much more readily than more dominant Aries types would be inclined to do. Reaching out towards the world, you are, nevertheless, somewhat locked inside yourself and can struggle to achieve the level of communication that you so desperately need. Frustration might easily follow, were it not for the fact that you possess a quiet determination that, to those in the know, is the clearest window through to your Aries soul.

The care for others is stronger here than with almost any other Aries type and you certainly demonstrate this at all levels. The fact is that you live a great percentage of your life in service to the people you take to, whilst at the same time being able to shut the door firmly in the face of people who irritate or anger you. You are deeply motivated towards family relationships.

Aries with Gemini Ascendant

A fairly jolly combination this, though by no means easy for others to come to terms with. You fly about from pillar to post and rarely stop long enough to take a breath. Admittedly this suits your own needs very well, but it can be a source of some disquiet to those around you, since they may not possess your energy or motivation. Those who know you well are deeply in awe of your capacity to keep going long after almost everyone else would have given up and gone home, though this quality is not always as wonderful as it sounds because it means that you put more pressure on your nervous system than just about any other astrological combination.

You need to be mindful of your nervous system, which responds to the erratic, mercurial quality of Gemini. Problems only really arise when the Aries part of you makes demands that the Gemini component finds difficult to deal with. There are paradoxes galore here and some of them need sorting out if you are ever fully to understand yourself, or are to be in a position when others know what makes you tick.

In relationships you might be a bit fickle, but you are a charmer and never stuck for the right words, no matter who you are dealing with. Your tenacity knows no bounds, though perhaps it should!

Aries with Cancer Ascendant

The main problem that you experience in life shows itself as a direct result of the meshing of these two very different zodiac signs. At heart Aries needs to dominate, whereas Cancer shows a desire to nurture. All too often the result can be a protective arm that is so strong that nobody could possibly get out from under it. Lighten your own load, and that of those you care for, by being willing to sit back and watch others please themselves a little. You might think that you know best, and your heart is clearly in the right place, but try to realise what life is like when someone is always on hand to tell you that they know better then you do.

But in a way this is a little severe, because you are fairly intuitive and your instincts would rarely lead you astray. Nobody could ask for a better partner or parent than you, though they might request a slightly less attentive one. In matters of work you are conscientious and are probably best suited to a job that means sorting out the kind of mess that humanity is so good at creating. You probably spend your spare time untangling balls of wool, though you are quite sporting too and could easily make the Olympics. Once there you would not win however, because you would be too concerned about all the other competitors.

Aries with Leo Ascendant

Here we come upon the first situation of Aries being allied with another Fire sign. This creates a character that could appear to be typically Aries at first sight and in many ways it is, though there are subtle differences that should not be ignored. Although you have the typical Aries ability to get things done, many of the tasks you do undertake will be for and on behalf of others. You can be proud, and on some occasions even haughty, and yet you are also regal in your bearing and honest to the point of absurdity. Nobody could doubt your sincerity and you have the soul of a poet combined with the courage of a lion.

All this is good, but it makes you rather difficult to approach, unless the person in question has first adopted a crouching and subservient attitude although you would not wish them to do so. It's simply that the impression you give and the motivation that underpins it are two quite different things. You are greatly respected and in the case of those individuals who know your real nature, you are also deeply loved. But life would be much simpler if you didn't always have to fight the wars that those around you are happy to start. Relaxation is a word that you don't really understand and you would do yourself a favour if you looked it up in a dictionary.

Aries with Virgo Ascendant

Virgo is steady and sure, though also fussy and stubborn. Aries is fast and determined, restless and active. It can already be seen that this is a rather strange meeting of characteristics and because Virgo is ruled by the capricious Mercury, the ultimate result will change from hour to hour and day to day. It isn't merely that others find it difficult to know where they are with you, they can't even understand what makes you tick. This will make you the subject of endless fascination and attention, at which you will be apparently surprised but inwardly pleased. If anyone ever really gets to know what goes on in that busy mind they may find the implications very difficult to deal with and it is a fact that only you would have the ability to live inside your crowded head.

As a partner and a parent you are second to none, though you tend to get on better with your children once they start to grow, since by this time you may be slightly less restricting to their own desires, which will often clash with your own on their behalf. You are capable of give and take and could certainly not be considered selfish, though your constant desire to get the best from everyone might occasionally be misconstrued.

Aries with Libra Ascendant

Libra has the tendency to bring out the best in any zodiac sign, and this is no exception when it comes together with Aries. You may, in fact, be the most comfortable of all Aries types, simply because Libra tempers some of your more assertive qualities and gives you the chance to balance out opposing forces, both inside yourself and in the world outside. You are fun to be with and make the staunchest friend possible. Although you are generally affable, few people would try to put one over on you, because they would quickly come to know how far you are willing to go before you let forth a string of invective that would shock those who previously underestimated your basic Aries traits.

Home and family are very dear to you, but you are more tolerant than some Aries types are inclined to be and you have a youthful zest for life that should stay with you no matter what age you manage to achieve. There is always something interesting to do and your mind is a constant stream of possibilities. This makes you very creative and you may also demonstrate a desire to look good at all times. You may not always be quite as confident as you appear to be, but few would guess the fact.

Aries with Scorpio Ascendant

The two very different faces of Mars come together in this potent, magnetic and quite awe-inspiring combination. Your natural inclination is towards secrecy and this fact, together with the natural attractions of the sensual Scorpio nature, makes you the object of great curiosity. This means that you will not go short of attention and should ensure that you are always being analysed by people who may never get to know you at all. At heart you prefer your own company, and yet life appears to find means to push you into the public gaze time and again. Most people with this combination ooze sex appeal and can use this fact as a stepping stone to personal success, yet without losing any integrity or loosening the cords of a deeply moralistic nature.

On those occasions when you do lose your temper, there isn't a character in the length and breadth of the zodiac who would have either the words or the courage to stand against the stream of invective that follows. On really rare occasions you might even scare yourself. As far as family members are concerned a simple look should be enough to show when you are not amused. Few people are left unmoved by your presence in their life.

Aries with Sagittarius Ascendant

What a lovely combination this can be, for the devil-may-care aspects of Sagittarius lighten the load of a sometimes too-serious Aries interior. Everything that glistens is not gold, though it's hard to convince you of the fact because, to mix metaphors, you can make a silk purse out of a sow's ear. Almost everyone loves you and in return you offer a friendship that is warm and protective, but not as demanding as sometimes tends to be the case with the Aries type. Relationships may be many and varied and there is often more than one major attachment in the life of those holding this combination. You will bring a breath of spring to any attachment, though you need to ensure that the person concerned is capable of keeping up with the hectic pace of your life.

It may appear from time to time that you are rather too trusting for your own good, though deep inside you are very astute and it seems that almost everything you undertake works out well in the end. This has nothing to do with native luck and is really down to the fact that you are much more calculating than might appear to be the case at first sight. As a parent you are protective yet offer sufficient room for self-expression.

Aries with Capricorn Ascendant

If ever anyone could be accused of setting off immediately, but slowly, it has to be you. These are very contradictory signs and the differences will express themselves in a variety of ways. One thing is certain, you have tremendous tenacity and will see a job through patiently from beginning to end, without tiring on the way, and ensuring that every detail is taken care of properly. This combination often bestows good health and a great capacity for continuity, particularly in terms of the length of life. You are certainly not as argumentative as the typical Aries, but you do know how to get your own way, which is just as well because you are usually thinking on behalf of everyone else and not just on your own account.

At home you can relax, which is a blessing for Aries, though in fact you seldom choose to do so because you always have some project or other on the go. You probably enjoy knocking down and rebuilding walls, though this is a practical tendency and not responsive to relationships, in which you are ardent and sincere. Impetuosity is as close to your heart as is the case for any type of Aries subject, though you certainly have the ability to appear patient and steady. But it's just a front, isn't it?

Aries with Aquarius Ascendant

The person standing on a soap box in the corner of the park, extolling the virtues of this or that, could quite easily be an Aries with an Aquarian Ascendant. You are certainly not averse to speaking your mind and you have plenty to talk about because you are the best social reformer and political animal of them all. Unorthodox in your approach, you have the ability to keep everyone guessing, except when it comes to getting your own way, for in this nobody doubts your natural abilities. You can put theories into practice very well and on the way you retain a sense of individuality that would shock more conservative types. It's true that a few people might find you a little difficult to approach and this is partly because you have an inner reserve and strength which is difficult for others to fathom.

In the world at large you take your place at the front, as any good Aquarian should, and yet you offer room for others to share your platform. You keep up with the latest innovations and treat family members as the genuine friends that you believe them to be. Care needs to be taken when picking a life partner, for you are an original, and not just anyone could match the peculiarities thrown up by this astrological combination.

Aries with Pisces Ascendant

Although not an easy combination to deal with, the Aries with a Piscean Ascendant does, nevertheless, bring something very special to the world in the way of natural understanding allied to practical assistance. It's true that you can sometimes be a dreamer, but there is nothing wrong with that as long as you have the ability to turn some of your wishes into reality, and this you are easily able to do, usually for the sake of those around you. Conversation comes easily to you, though you also possess a slightly wistful and poetic side to your nature, which is attractive to the many people who call you a friend. A natural entertainer, you bring a sense of the comic to the often serious qualities of Aries, though without losing the determination that typifies the sign.

In relationships you are ardent, sincere and supportive, with a strong social conscience that sometimes finds you fighting the battles of the less privileged members of society. Family is important to you and this is a combination that invariably leads to parenthood. Away from the cut and thrust of everyday life you relax more fully and think about matters more deeply than more typical Aries types might.

THE MOON AND THE PART IT PLAYS IN YOUR LIFE

In astrology the Moon is probably the single most important heavenly body after the Sun. Its unique position, as partner to the Earth on its journey around the solar system, means that the Moon appears to pass through the signs of the zodiac extremely quickly. The zodiac position of the Moon at the time of your birth plays a great part in personal character and is especially significant in the build-up of your emotional nature.

Your Own Moon Sign

Discovering the position of the Moon at the time of your birth has always been notoriously difficult because tracking the complex zodiac positions of the Moon is not easy. This process has been reduced to three simple stages with our Lunar Tables. A breakdown of the Moon's zodiac positions can be found from page 35 onwards, so that once you know what your Moon Sign is, you can see what part this plays in the overall build-up of your personal character.

If you follow the instructions on the next page you will soon be able to work out exactly what zodiac sign the Moon occupied on the day that you were born and you can then go on to compare the reading for this position with those of your Sun sign and your Ascendant. It is partly the comparison between these three important positions that goes towards making you the unique individual you are.

How To Discover Your Moon Sign

This is a three-stage process. You may need a pen and a piece of paper but if you follow the instructions below the process should only take a minute or so.

STAGE 1 First of all you need to know the Moon Age at the time of your birth. If you look at Moon Table 1, on page 33, you will find all the years between 1921 and 2019 down the left side. Find the year of your birth and then trace across to the right to the month of your birth. Where the two intersect you will find a number. This is the date of the New Moon in the month that you were born. You now need to count forward the number of days between the New Moon and your own birthday. For example, if the New Moon in the month of your birth was shown as being the 6th and you were born on the 20th, your Moon Age Day would be 14. If the New Moon in the month of your birth came after your birthday, you need to count forward from the New Moon in the previous month. If you were born in a Leap Year, remember to count the 29th February. You can tell if your birth year was a Leap Year if the last two digits can be divided by four. Whatever the result, jot this number down so that you do not forget it.

STAGE 2 Take a look at Moon Table 2 on page 34. Down the left hand column look for the date of your birth. Now trace across to the month of your birth. Where the two meet you will find a letter. Copy this letter down alongside your Moon Age Day.

STAGE 3 Moon Table 3 on page 34 will supply you with the zodiac sign the Moon occupied on the day of your birth. Look for your Moon Age Day down the left hand column and then for the letter you found in Stage 2. Where the two converge you will find a zodiac sign and this is the sign occupied by the Moon on the day that you were born.

Your Zodiac Moon Sign Explained

You will find a profile of all zodiac Moon Signs on pages 35 to 38, showing in yet another way how astrology helps to make you into the individual that you are. In each daily entry of the Astral Diary you can find the zodiac position of the Moon for every day of the year. This also allows you to discover your lunar birthdays. Since the Moon passes through all the signs of the zodiac in about a month, you can expect something like twelve lunar birthdays each year. At these times you are likely to be emotionally steady and able to make the sort of decisions that have real, lasting value.

MOON TABLE 1

YEAR	FEB	MAR	APR	YEAR	FEB	MAR	APR	YEAR	FEB	MAR	APR
1921	8	9	8	1954	3	5	3	1987	28	29	28
1922	26	28	27	1955	22	24	22	1988	17	18	16
1923	15	17	16	1956	11	12	11	1989	6	7	6
1924	5	5	4	1957	–	1/31	29	1990	25	26	25
1925	23	24	23	1958	18	20	19	1991	14	15	13
1926	12	14	12	1959	7	9	8	1992	3	4	3
1927	2	3	2	1960	26	27	26	1993	22	24	22
1928	19	21	20	1961	15	16	15	1994	10	12	11
1929	9	11	9	1962	5	6	5	1995	29	30	29
1930	28	30	28	1963	23	25	23	1996	18	19	18
1931	17	19	18	1964	13	14	12	1997	7	9	7
1932	6	7	6	1965	1	2	1	1998	26	27	26
1933	24	26	24	1966	19	21	20	1999	16	17	16
1934	14	15	13	1967	9	10	9	2000	5	6	4
1935	3	5	3	1968	28	29	28	2001	23	24	23
1936	22	23	21	1969	17	18	16	2002	12	13	12
1937	11	13	12	1970	6	7	6	2003	–	2	1
1938	–	2/31	30	1971	25	26	25	2004	20	21	19
1939	19	20	19	1972	14	15	13	2005	9	10	8
1940	8	9	7	1973	4	5	3	2006	28	29	27
1941	26	27	26	1974	22	24	22	2007	15	18	17
1942	15	16	15	1975	11	12	11	2008	6	7	6
1943	4	6	4	1976	29	30	29	2009	25	26	25
1944	24	24	22	1977	18	19	18	2010	14	15	14
1945	12	14	12	1978	7	9	7	2011	3	5	3
1946	2	3	2	1979	26	27	26	2012	22	22	21
1947	19	21	20	1980	15	16	15	2013	10	12	10
1948	9	11	9	1981	4	6	4	2014	1	1/31	30
1949	27	29	28	1982	23	24	23	2015	19	20	19
1950	16	18	17	1983	13	14	13	2016	8	8	7
1951	6	7	6	1984	1	2	1	2017	25	27	25
1952	25	25	24	1985	19	21	20	2018	15	17	16
1953	14	15	13	1986	9	10	9	2019	6	5	4

TABLE 2 MOON TABLE 3

DAY	MAR	APR	M/D	F	G	H	I	J	K	L
1	F	J	0	PI	PI	AR	AR	AR	TA	TA
2	G	J	1	PI	AR	AR	AR	TA	TA	TA
3	G	J	2	AR	AR	AR	TA	TA	TA	GE
4	G	J	3	AR	AR	TA	TA	TA	GE	GE
5	G	J	4	AR	TA	TA	GE	GE	GE	GE
6	G	J	5	TA	TA	GE	GE	GE	CA	CA
7	G	J	6	TA	GE	GE	GE	CA	CA	CA
8	G	J	7	GE	GE	GE	CA	CA	CA	LE
9	G	J	8	GE	GE	CA	CA	CA	LE	LE
10	G	J	9	CA	CA	CA	CA	LE	LE	VI
11	G	K	10	CA	CA	LE	LE	LE	VI	VI
12	H	K	11	CA	LE	LE	LE	VI	VI	VI
13	H	K	12	LE	LE	LE	VI	VI	VI	LI
14	H	K	13	LE	LE	VI	VI	VI	LI	LI
15	H	K	14	VI	VI	VI	LI	LI	LI	LI
16	H	K	15	VI	VI	LI	LI	LI	SC	SC
17	H	K	16	VI	LI	LI	LI	SC	SC	SC
18	H	K	17	LI	LI	LI	SC	SC	SC	SA
19	H	K	18	LI	LI	SC	SC	SC	SA	SA
20	H	K	19	LI	SC	SC	SC	SA	SA	SA
21	H	L	20	SC	SC	SA	SA	SA	CP	CP
22	I	L	21	SC	SA	SA	SA	CP	CP	CP
23	I	L	22	SC	SA	SA	CP	CP	CP	AQ
24	I	L	23	SA	SA	CP	CP	CP	AQ	AQ
25	I	L	24	SA	CP	CP	CP	AQ	AQ	AQ
26	I	L	25	CP	CP	AQ	AQ	AQ	PI	PI
27	I	L	26	CP	AQ	AQ	AQ	PI	PI	PI
28	I	L	27	AQ	AQ	AQ	PI	PI	PI	AR
29	I	L	28	AQ	AQ	PI	PI	PI	AR	AR
30	I	L	29	AQ	PI	PI	PI	AR	AR	AR
31	I	–								

AR = Aries, TA = Taurus, GE = Gemini, CA = Cancer, LE = Leo, VI = Virgo,
LI = Libra, SC = Scorpio, SA = Sagittarius, CP = Capricorn, AQ = Aquarius, PI = Pisces

MOON SIGNS

Moon in Aries

You have a strong imagination, courage, determination and a desire to do things in your own way and forge your own path through life.

Originality is a key attribute; you are seldom stuck for ideas although your mind is changeable and you could take the time to focus on individual tasks. Often quick-tempered, you take orders from few people and live life at a fast pace. Avoid health problems by taking regular time out for rest and relaxation.

Emotionally, it is important that you talk to those you are closest to and work out your true feelings. Once you discover that people are there to help, there is less necessity for you to do everything yourself.

Moon in Taurus

The Moon in Taurus gives you a courteous and friendly manner, which means you are likely to have many friends.

The good things in life mean a lot to you, as Taurus is an Earth sign that delights in experiences which please the senses. Hence you are probably a lover of good food and drink, which may in turn mean you need to keep an eye on the bathroom scales, especially as looking good is also important to you.

Emotionally you are fairly stable and you stick by your own standards. Taureans do not respond well to change. Intuition also plays an important part in your life.

Moon in Gemini

You have a warm-hearted character, sympathetic and eager to help others. At times reserved, you can also be articulate and chatty: this is part of the paradox of Gemini, which always brings duplicity to the nature. You are interested in current affairs, have a good intellect, and are good company and likely to have many friends. Most of your friends have a high opinion of you and would be ready to defend you should the need arise. However, this is usually unnecessary, as you are quite capable of defending yourself in any verbal confrontation.

Travel is important to your inquisitive mind and you find intellectual stimulus in mixing with people from different cultures. You also gain much from reading, writing and the arts but you do need plenty of rest and relaxation in order to avoid fatigue.

Moon in Cancer

The Moon in Cancer at the time of birth is a fortunate position as Cancer is the Moon's natural home. This means that the qualities of compassion and understanding given by the Moon are especially enhanced in your nature, and you are friendly and sociable and cope well with emotional pressures. You cherish home and family life, and happily do the domestic tasks. Your surroundings are important to you and you hate squalor and filth. You are likely to have a love of music and poetry.

Your basic character, although at times changeable like the Moon itself, depends on symmetry. You aim to make your surroundings comfortable and harmonious, for yourself and those close to you.

Moon in Leo

The best qualities of the Moon and Leo come together to make you warm-hearted, fair, ambitious and self-confident. With good organisational abilities, you invariably rise to a position of responsibility in your chosen career. This is fortunate as you don't enjoy being an 'also-ran' and would rather be an important part of a small organisation than a menial in a large one.

You should be lucky in love, and happy, provided you put in the effort to make a comfortable home for yourself and those close to you. It is likely that you will have a love of pleasure, sport, music and literature. Life brings you many rewards, most of them as a direct result of your own efforts, although you may be luckier than average and ready to make the best of any situation.

Moon in Virgo

You are endowed with good mental abilities and a keen receptive memory, but you are never ostentatious or pretentious. Naturally quite reserved, you still have many friends, especially of the opposite sex. Marital relationships must be discussed carefully and worked at so that they remain harmonious, as personal attachments can be a problem if you do not give them your full attention.

Talented and persevering, you possess artistic qualities and are a good homemaker. Earning your honours through genuine merit, you work long and hard towards your objectives but show little pride in your achievements. Many short journeys will be undertaken in your life.

Moon in Libra

With the Moon in Libra you are naturally popular and make friends easily. People like you, probably more than you realise, you bring fun to a party and are a natural diplomat. For all its good points, Libra is not the most stable of astrological signs and, as a result, your emotions can be a little unstable too. Therefore, although the Moon in Libra is said to be good for love and marriage, your Sun sign and Rising sign will have an important effect on your emotional and loving qualities.

You must remember to relate to others in your decision-making. Co-operation is crucial because Libra represents the 'balance' of life that can only be achieved through harmonious relationships. Conformity is not easy for you because Libra, an Air sign, likes its independence.

Moon in Scorpio

Some people might call you pushy. In fact, all you really want to do is to live life to the full and protect yourself and your family from the pressures of life. Take care to avoid giving the impression of being sarcastic or impulsive and use your energies wisely and constructively.

You have great courage and you invariably achieve your goals by force of personality and sheer effort. You are fond of mystery and are good at predicting the outcome of situations and events. Travel experiences can be beneficial to you.

You may experience problems if you do not take time to examine your motives in a relationship, and also if you allow jealousy, always a feature of Scorpio, to cloud your judgement.

Moon in Sagittarius

The Moon in Sagittarius helps to make you a generous individual with humanitarian qualities and a kind heart. Restlessness may be intrinsic as your mind is seldom still. Perhaps because of this, you have a need for change that could lead you to several major moves during your adult life. You are not afraid to stand your ground when you know your judgement is right, you speak directly and have good intuition.

At work you are quick, efficient and versatile and so you make an ideal employee. You need work to be intellectually demanding and do not enjoy tedious routines.

In relationships, you anger quickly if faced with stupidity or deception, though you are just as quick to forgive and forget. Emotionally, there are times when your heart rules your head.

37

Moon in Capricorn

The Moon in Capricorn makes you popular and likely to come into the public eye in some way. The watery Moon is not entirely comfortable in the Earth sign of Capricorn and this may lead to some difficulties in the early years of life. An initial lack of creative ability and indecision must be overcome before the true qualities of patience and perseverance inherent in Capricorn can show through.

You have good administrative ability and are a capable worker, and if you are careful you can accumulate wealth. But you must be cautious and take professional advice in partnerships, as you are open to deception. You may be interested in social or welfare work, which suit your organisational skills and sympathy for others.

Moon in Aquarius

The Moon in Aquarius makes you an active and agreeable person with a friendly, easy-going nature. Sympathetic to the needs of others, you flourish in a laid-back atmosphere. You are broad-minded, fair and open to suggestion, although sometimes you have an unconventional quality which others can find hard to understand.

You are interested in the strange and curious, and in old articles and places. You enjoy trips to these places and gain much from them. Political, scientific and educational work interests you and you might choose a career in science or technology.

Money-wise, you make gains through innovation and concentration and Lunar Aquarians often tackle more than one job at a time. In love you are kind and honest.

Moon in Pisces

You have a kind, sympathetic nature, somewhat retiring at times, but you always take account of others' feelings and help when you can.

Personal relationships may be problematic, but as life goes on you can learn from your experiences and develop a better understanding of yourself and the world around you.

You have a fondness for travel, appreciate beauty and harmony and hate disorder and strife. You may be fond of literature and would make a good writer or speaker yourself. You have a creative imagination and may come across as an incurable romantic. You have strong intuition, maybe bordering on a mediumistic quality, which sets you apart from the mass. You may not be rich in cash terms, but your personal gifts are worth more than gold.

ARIES IN LOVE

Discover how compatible in love you are with people from the same and other signs of the zodiac. Five stars equals a match made in heaven!

Aries meets Aries

This could be an all-or-nothing pairing. Both parties are from a dominant sign, so someone will have to be flexible in order to maintain personal harmony. Both know what they want out of life, and may have trouble overcoming any obstacles a relationship creates. This is a good physical pairing, with a chemistry that few other matches enjoy to the same level. Attitude is everything, but at least there is a mutual admiration that makes gazing at your partner like looking in the mirror. Star rating: ****

Aries meets Taurus

This is a match that has been known to work very well. Aries brings dynamism and ambition, while Taurus has the patience to see things through logically. Such complementary views work equally well in a relationship or in the office. There is mutual respect, but sometimes a lack of total understanding. The romantic needs of each are quite different, but both are still fulfilled. They can live easily in domestic harmony which is very important but, interestingly, Aries may be the loser in battles of will. Star rating: ***

Aries meets Gemini

Don't expect peace and harmony with this combination, although what comes along instead might make up for any disagreements. Gemini has a very fertile imagination, while Aries has the tenacity to make reality from fantasy. Combined, they have a sizzling relationship. There are times when both parties could explode with indignation and something has to give. But even if there are clashes, making them up will always be most enjoyable! Mutual financial success is likely in this match. Star rating: ****

Aries meets Cancer

A potentially one-sided pairing, it often appears that the Cancerian is brow-beaten by the far more dominant Arian. So much depends on the patience of the Cancerian individual, because if good psychology is present – who knows? But beware, Aries, you may find your partner too passive, and constantly having to take the lead can be wearing – even for you. A prolonged trial period would be advantageous, as the match could easily go either way. When it does work, though, this relationship is usually contented. Star rating: ***

Aries meets Leo

Stand by for action and make sure the house is sound-proof. Leo is a lofty idealist and there is always likely to be friction when two Fire signs meet. To compensate, there is much mutual admiration, together with a desire to please. Where there are shared incentives, the prognosis is good but it's important not to let little irritations blow up. Both signs want to have their own way and this is a sure cause of trouble. There might not be much patience here, but there is plenty of action. Star rating: *****

Aries meets Virgo

Neither of these signs really understands the other, and that could easily lead to a clash. Virgo is so pedantic, which will drive Aries up the wall, while Aries always wants to be moving on to the next objective, before Virgo is even settled with the last one. It will take time for these two to get to know each other, but this is a great business matching. If a personal relationship is seen in these terms then the prognosis can be good, but on the whole, this is not an inspiring match. Star rating: ***

Aries meets Libra

These signs are zodiac opposites which means a make-or-break situation. The match will either be a great success or a dismal failure. Why? Well Aries finds it difficult to understand the flighty Air-sign tendencies of Libra, whilst the natural balance of Libra contradicts the unorthodox Arian methods. Any flexibility will come from Libra, which may mean that things work out for a while, but Libra only has so much patience and it may eventually run out. In the end, Aries may be just too bossy for an independent but sensitive sign like Libra. Star rating: **

Aries meets Scorpio

There can be great affection here, even if the two zodiac signs are so very different. The common link is the planet Mars, which plays a part in both these natures. Although Aries is, outwardly, the most dominant, Scorpio people are among the most powerful to be found anywhere. This quiet determination is respected by Aries. Aries will satisfy the passionate side of Scorpio, particularly with instruction from Scorpio. There are mysteries here which will add spice to life. The few arguments that do occur are likely to be awe-inspiring. Star rating: ****

Aries meets Sagittarius

This can be one of the most favourable matches of them all. Both Aries and Sagittarius are Fire signs, which often leads to clashes of will, but this pair find a mutual understanding. Sagittarius helps Aries to develop a better sense of humour, while Aries teaches the Archer about consistency on the road to success. Some patience is called for on both sides, but these people have a natural liking for each other. Add this to growing love and you have a long-lasting combination that is hard to beat. Star rating: *****

Aries meets Capricorn

Capricorn works conscientiously to achieve its objectives and so can be the perfect companion for Aries. The Ram knows how to achieve but not how to consolidate, so the two signs have a great deal to offer one another practically. There may not be fireworks and it's sometimes doubtful how well they know each other, but it may not matter. Aries is outwardly hot but inwardly cool, whilst Capricorn can appear low key but be a furnace underneath. Such a pairing can gradually find contentment, though both parties may wonder how this is so. Star rating: ****

Aries meets Aquarius

Aquarius is an Air sign, and Air and Fire often work well together, but perhaps not in the case of Aries and Aquarius. The average Aquarian lives in what the Ram sees as a fantasy world, so without a sufficiently good meeting of minds, compromise may be lacking. Of course, almost anything is possible, and the dominant side of Aries could be trained by the devil-may-care attitude of Aquarius. There are meeting points but they are difficult to establish. However, given sufficient time and an open mind on both sides, a degree of happiness is possible. Star rating: **

Aries meets Pisces

Still waters run deep, and they don't come much deeper than Pisces. Although these signs share the same quadrant of the zodiac, they have little in common. Pisces is a dreamer, a romantic idealist with steady and spiritual goals. Aries needs to be on the move, and has very different ideals. It's hard to see how a relationship could develop because the outlook on life is so different but, with patience, especially from Aries, there is a chance that things might work out. Pisces needs incentive, and Aries may be the sign to offer it. Star rating: **

VENUS:
THE PLANET OF LOVE

If you look up at the sky around sunset or sunrise you will often see Venus in close attendance to the Sun. It is arguably one of the most beautiful sights of all and there is little wonder that historically it became associated with the goddess of love. But although Venus does play an important part in the way you view love and in the way others see you romantically, this is only one of the spheres of influence that it enjoys in your overall character.

Venus has a part to play in the more cultured side of your life and has much to do with your appreciation of art, literature, music and general creativity. Even the way you look is responsive to the part of the zodiac that Venus occupied at the start of your life, though this fact is also down to your Sun sign and Ascending sign. If, at the time you were born, Venus occupied one of the more gregarious zodiac signs, you will be more likely to wear your heart on your sleeve, as well as to be more attracted to entertainment, social gatherings and good company. If on the other hand Venus occupied a quiet zodiac sign at the time of your birth, you would tend to be more retiring and less willing to shine in public situations.

It's good to know what part the planet Venus plays in your life for it can have a great bearing on the way you appear to the rest of the world and since we all have to mix with others, you can learn to make the very best of what Venus has to offer you.

One of the great complications in the past has always been trying to establish exactly what zodiac position Venus enjoyed when you were born because the planet is notoriously difficult to track. However, we have solved that problem by creating a table that is exclusive to your Sun sign, which you will find on the following page.

Establishing your Venus sign could not be easier. Just look up the year of your birth on the following page and you will see a sign of the zodiac. This was the sign that Venus occupied in the period covered by your sign in that year. If Venus occupied more than one sign during the period, this is indicated by the date on which the sign changed, and the name of the new sign. For instance, if you were born in 1950, Venus was in Aquarius until the 7th April, after which time it was in Pisces. If you were born before 7th April your Venus sign is Aquarius, if you were born on or after 7th April, your Venus sign is Pisces. Once you have established the position of Venus at the time of your birth, you can then look in the pages which follow to see how this has a bearing on your life as a whole.

1921 TAURUS
1922 ARIES / 13.4 TAURUS
1923 AQUARIUS / 1.4 PISCES
1924 TAURUS / 6.4 GEMINI
1925 PISCES / 28.3 ARIES
1926 AQUARIUS / 6.4 PISCES
1927 ARIES / 24.3 TAURUS
1928 PISCES / 13.4 ARIES
1929 TAURUS / 20.4 ARIES
1930 ARIES / 13.4 TAURUS
1931 AQUARIUS / 31.3 PISCES
1932 TAURUS / 6.4 GEMINI
1933 PISCES / 27.3 ARIES
1934 AQUARIUS / 6.4 PISCES
1935 ARIES / 23.3 TAURUS
1936 PISCES / 13.4 ARIES
1937 TAURUS / 14.4 ARIES
1938 ARIES / 12.4 TAURUS
1939 AQUARIUS / 31.3 PISCES
1940 TAURUS / 5.4 GEMINI
1941 PISCES / 26.3 ARIES /
    20.4 TAURUS
1942 AQUARIUS / 7.4 PISCES
1943 ARIES / 23.3 TAURUS
1944 PISCES / 12.4 ARIES
1945 TAURUS / 8.4 ARIES
1946 ARIES / 12.4 TAURUS
1947 AQUARIUS / 30.3 PISCES
1948 TAURUS / 5.4 GEMINI
1949 PISCES / 25.3 ARIES /
    20.4 TAURUS
1950 AQUARIUS / 7.4 PISCES
1951 ARIES / 22.3 TAURUS
1952 PISCES / 12.4 ARIES
1953 TAURUS / 1.4 ARIES
1954 ARIES / 11.4 TAURUS
1955 AQUARIUS / 30.3 PISCES
1956 TAURUS / 4.4 GEMINI
1957 PISCES / 25.3 ARIES /
    19.4 TAURUS
1958 AQUARIUS / 8.4 PISCES
1959 ARIES / 22.3 TAURUS
1960 PISCES / 11.4 ARIES
1961 ARIES
1962 ARIES / 11.4 TAURUS
1963 AQUARIUS / 29.3 PISCES
1964 TAURUS / 4.4 GEMINI
1965 PISCES / 24.3 ARIES /
    19.4 TAURUS
1966 AQUARIUS / 8.4 PISCES
1967 TAURUS / 20.4 GEMINI
1968 PISCES / 10.4 ARIES
1969 ARIES
1970 ARIES / 10.4 TAURUS

1971 AQUARIUS / 29.3 PISCES
1972 TAURUS / 3.4 GEMINI
1973 PISCES / 24.3 ARIES /
    18.4 TAURUS
1974 AQUARIUS / 8.4 PISCES
1975 TAURUS / 19.4 GEMINI
1976 PISCES / 10.4 ARIES
1977 ARIES
1978 ARIES / 10.4 TAURUS
1979 AQUARIUS / 28.3 PISCES
1980 TAURUS / 3.4 GEMINI
1981 PISCES / 23.3 ARIES /
    18.4 TAURUS
1982 AQUARIUS / 9.4 PISCES
1983 TAURUS / 19.4 GEMINI
1984 PISCES / 9.4 ARIES
1985 ARIES
1986 ARIES / 9.4 TAURUS
1987 AQUARIUS / 28.3 PISCES
1988 TAURUS / 2.4 GEMINI
1989 PISCES / 23.3 ARIES /
    17.4 TAURUS
1990 AQUARIUS / 9.4 PISCES
1991 TAURUS / 18.4 GEMINI
1992 PISCES / 9.4 ARIES
1993 ARIES
1994 ARIES / 9.4 TAURUS
1995 AQUARIUS / 27.3 PISCES
1996 TAURUS / 2.4 GEMINI
1997 PISCES / 22.3 ARIES /
    17.4 TAURUS
1998 AQUARIUS / 9.4 PISCES
1999 TAURUS / 18.4 GEMINI
2000 PISCES / 9.4 ARIES
2001 ARIES
2002 ARIES / 7.4 TAURUS
2003 AQUARIUS / 27.3 PISCES
2004 TAURUS / 1.4 GEMINI
2005 PISCES/22.3 ARIES
2006 AQUARIUS/7.4 PISCES
2007 TAURUS / 16.4 GEMINI
2008 PISCES / 9.4 ARIES
2009 ARIES
2010 ARIES / 7.4 TAURUS
2011 AQUARIUS / 27.3 PISCES
2012 TAURUS / 1.4 GEMINI
2013 PISCES / 22.3 ARIES
2014 AQUARIUS / 7.4 PISCES
2015 TAURUS / 16.4 GEMINI
2016 PISCES / 9.4 ARIES
2017 TAURUS / 1.4 GEMINI
2018 ARIES / 7.4 TAURUS
2019 AQUARIUS / 27.3 PISCES

VENUS THROUGH THE ZODIAC SIGNS

Venus in Aries

Amongst other things, the position of Venus in Aries indicates a fondness for travel, music and all creative pursuits. Your nature tends to be affectionate and you would try not to create confusion or difficulty for others if it could be avoided. Many people with this planetary position have a great love of the theatre, and mental stimulation is of the greatest importance. Early romantic attachments are common with Venus in Aries, so it is very important to establish a genuine sense of romantic continuity. Early marriage is not recommended, especially if it is based on sympathy. You may give your heart a little too readily on occasions.

Venus in Taurus

You are capable of very deep feelings and your emotions tend to last for a very long time. This makes you a trusting partner and lover, whose constancy is second to none. In life you are precise and careful and always try to do things the right way. Although this means an ordered life, which you are comfortable with, it can also lead you to be rather too fussy for your own good. Despite your pleasant nature, you are very fixed in your opinions and quite able to speak your mind. Others are attracted to you and historical astrologers always quoted this position of Venus as being very fortunate in terms of marriage. However, if you find yourself involved in a failed relationship, it could take you a long time to trust again.

Venus in Gemini

As with all associations related to Gemini, you tend to be quite versatile, anxious for change and intelligent in your dealings with the world at large. You may gain money from more than one source but you are equally good at spending it. There is an inference here that you are a good communicator, via either the written or the spoken word, and you love to be in the company of interesting people. Always on the look-out for culture, you may also be very fond of music, and love to indulge the curious and cultured side of your nature. In romance you tend to have more than one relationship and could find yourself associated with someone who has previously been a friend or even a distant relative.

Venus in Cancer

You often stay close to home because you are very fond of family and enjoy many of your most treasured moments when you are with those you love. Being naturally sympathetic, you will always do anything you can to support those around you, even people you hardly know at all. This charitable side of your nature is your most noticeable trait and is one of the reasons why others are naturally so fond of you. Being receptive and in some cases even psychic, you can see through to the soul of most of those with whom you come into contact. You may not commence too many romantic attachments but when you do give your heart, it tends to be unconditionally.

Venus in Leo

It must become quickly obvious to almost anyone you meet that you are kind, sympathetic and yet determined enough to stand up for anyone or anything that is truly important to you. Bright and sunny, you warm the world with your natural enthusiasm and would rarely do anything to hurt those around you, or at least not intentionally. In romance you are ardent and sincere, though some may find your style just a little overpowering. Gains come through your contacts with other people and this could be especially true with regard to romance, for love and money often come hand in hand for those who were born with Venus in Leo. People claim to understand you, though you are more complex than you seem.

Venus in Virgo

Your nature could well be fairly quiet no matter what your Sun sign might be, though this fact often manifests itself as an inner peace and would not prevent you from being basically sociable. Some delays and even the odd disappointment in love cannot be ruled out with this planetary position, though it's a fact that you will usually find the happiness you look for in the end. Catapulting yourself into romantic entanglements that you know to be rather ill-advised is not sensible, and it would be better to wait before you committed yourself exclusively to any one person. It is the essence of your nature to serve the world at large and through doing so it is possible that you will attract money at some stage in your life.

Venus in Libra

Venus is very comfortable in Libra and bestows upon those people who have this planetary position a particular sort of kindness that is easy to recognise. This is a very good position for all sorts of friendships and also for romantic attachments that usually bring much joy into your life. Few individuals with Venus in Libra would avoid marriage and since you are capable of great depths of love, it is likely that you will find a contented personal life. You like to mix with people of integrity and intelligence but don't take kindly to scruffy surroundings or work that means getting your hands too dirty. Careful speculation, good business dealings and money through marriage all seem fairly likely.

Venus in Scorpio

You are quite open and tend to spend money quite freely, even on those occasions when you don't have very much. Although your intentions are always good, there are times when you get yourself into the odd scrape and this can be particularly true when it comes to romance, which you may come to late or from a rather unexpected direction. Certainly you have the power to be happy and to make others contented on the way, but you find the odd stumbling block on your journey through life and it could seem that you have to work harder than those around you. As a result of this, you gain a much deeper understanding of the true value of personal happiness than many people ever do, and are likely to achieve true contentment in the end.

Venus in Sagittarius

You are lighthearted, cheerful and always able to see the funny side of any situation. These facts enhance your popularity, which is especially high with members of the opposite sex. You should never have to look too far to find romantic interest in your life, though it is just possible that you might be too willing to commit yourself before you are certain that the person in question is right for you. Part of the problem here extends to other areas of life too. The fact is that you like variety in everything and so can tire of situations that fail to offer it. All the same, if you choose wisely and learn to understand your restless side, then great happiness can be yours.

Venus in Capricorn

The most notable trait that comes from Venus in this position is that it makes you trustworthy and able to take on all sorts of responsibilities in life. People are instinctively fond of you and love you all the more because you are always ready to help those who are in any form of need. Social and business popularity can be yours and there is a magnetic quality to your nature that is particularly attractive in a romantic sense. Anyone who wants a partner for a lover, a spouse and a good friend too would almost certainly look in your direction. Constancy is the hallmark of your nature and unfaithfulness would go right against the grain. You might sometimes be a little too trusting.

Venus in Aquarius

This location of Venus offers a fondness for travel and a desire to try out something new at every possible opportunity. You are extremely easy to get along with and tend to have many friends from varied backgrounds, classes and inclinations. You like to live a distinct sort of life and gain a great deal from moving about, both in a career sense and with regard to your home. It is not out of the question that you could form a romantic attachment to someone who comes from far away or be attracted to a person of a distinctly artistic and original nature. What you cannot stand is jealousy, for you have friends of both sexes and would want to keep things that way.

Venus in Pisces

The first thing people tend to notice about you is your wonderful, warm smile. Being very charitable by nature you will do anything to help others, even if you don't know them well. Much of your life may be spent sorting out situations for other people, but it is very important to feel that you are living for yourself too. In the main, you remain cheerful, and tend to be quite attractive to members of the opposite sex. Where romantic attachments are concerned, you could be drawn to people who are significantly older or younger than yourself or to someone with a unique career or point of view. It might be best for you to avoid marrying whilst you are still very young.

ARIES:
2018 DIARY PAGES

October

2018

1 MONDAY
Moon Age Day 22   Moon Sign Gemini

You want to create a pleasant environment for everyone and won't take kindly to people who show a desire to upset the applecart in any way. However, it is important to keep your temper and not to allow yourself to rise to any bait that is being deliberately dangled by someone who may not like you very much.

2 TUESDAY
Moon Age Day 23   Moon Sign Cancer

The ability to mix business with pleasure is the great forte of your zodiac sign and this fact really shows today. The accent now is clearly on romance and fun. You can perfect your creative skills in organising gatherings or social functions, whilst at the same time feathering your nest in more practical ways.

3 WEDNESDAY
Moon Age Day 24   Moon Sign Cancer

Although you might feel a great sense of freedom around now, you won't be all that keen to travel further than is strictly necessary. Concentrate today on more emotional or even spiritual matters, since the arrival of this particular Wednesday should bring more time to stand aside from the purely practical aspects of life.

4 THURSDAY
Moon Age Day 25   Moon Sign Leo

New relationships could be on the cards for Arians who have been looking for love and you won't have any difficulty at all charming the birds down from the trees, either now or tomorrow. Romantically and personally, today should mark one of the most enjoyable times during the whole of October.

5 FRIDAY   *Moon Age Day 26   Moon Sign Leo*

Today should find you quite contented. There is a strong sense of togetherness around, which is especially emphasised in your love life today. Relating to people from your past should now also be easier and you might be in a position to bury a hatchet that has been a problem for some time. Arbitrating between others is also possible.

6 SATURDAY   *Moon Age Day 27   Moon Sign Virgo*

Don't let yourself become upset about matters in the wider family, some of which appear to be giving you a slightly hard time today. It is close partnerships that make life most fulfilling now, both in a romantic sense and for those who are in co-operative professional ventures. Focus on these areas until tension in others dissipates.

7 SUNDAY   *Moon Age Day 28   Moon Sign Virgo*

Someone you haven't seen for ages could be visiting your life again today. Listen to what others are saying, especially your life partner. He or she is likely to have some very good ideas at present. These, taken together with your own ability to make reality from fantasy, prove to be extremely important in your life right now.

8 MONDAY   *Moon Age Day 29   Moon Sign Virgo*

Aries is sometimes accused of being selfish, though the truth is that you are merely single-minded. Having said this, it wouldn't do any harm today to remember that there are other people involved in your decisions. It is possible that you are thinking of number one at the beginning of this working week – and this is never a good idea if it blinds you to those around you.

9 TUESDAY   *Moon Age Day 0   Moon Sign Libra*

The arrival of the lunar low will probably coincide with a less-active phase that will continue for a couple more days. Be careful whom you trust today. Even though your instincts right now are to give others the benefit of the doubt, there are one or two people around at present that may not be what they seem.

10 WEDNESDAY *Moon Age Day 1   Moon Sign Libra*

Avoid being too quick to jump to conclusions, and a degree of circumspection would also be sensible. There are advantages to looking at specific situations in isolation around now. This Wednesday brings a desire to spend time with family members and to do something you see as being essentially interesting.

11 THURSDAY *Moon Age Day 2   Moon Sign Scorpio*

This ought to be a bright and breezy sort of day, without too much in the way of perceived responsibility but with plenty of entertainment and fun. The friendly assistance that comes from the direction of people you know, as well as strangers, is bound to be especially well received today.

12 FRIDAY *Moon Age Day 3   Moon Sign Scorpio*

It isn't the things you want to do that matter right now but rather the things you have to do. As long as you keep a smile on your face, the day should prove to be a breeze. Professional matters are likely to go more smoothly today, even if in your heart you would rather be somewhere else.

13 SATURDAY *Moon Age Day 4   Moon Sign Sagittarius*

Not much ruffles your feathers at the moment, though you won't take too kindly to being told what to do. This only really applies if you work on a Saturday. Most home-based situations ought to prove distinctly relaxing, so your main focus today is likely to be on your domestic life. Enjoy the chance to put yourself first for once!

14 SUNDAY *Moon Age Day 5   Moon Sign Sagittarius*

Perhaps you are slightly more considerate than usual regarding the feelings of those around you. Aries is becoming quite creative around now, perhaps leading to a decorating spree at home. Social and teamwork matters are favourably highlighted now, and these trends suggest that you will be getting on well with the world.

15 MONDAY   *Moon Age Day 6   Moon Sign Capricorn*

Not everything interests you today, but lots will. Getting to know others can be extraordinarily fascinating, particularly when you are dealing with people who have a mysterious fascination of some sort. Along comes a period of high enthusiasm and a time when you are showing your best face to the world at large.

16 TUESDAY   *Moon Age Day 7   Moon Sign Capricorn*

The impact of your personality remains generally strong, so it isn't hard to get what you want from life, or to influence people along the way. Romance is a possibility, and if you are single this could perhaps be coming from an unexpected direction. Alternatively, an old flame could be rekindled before the weekend.

17 WEDNESDAY   *Moon Age Day 8   Moon Sign Capricorn*

Although things are getting better and better from a social point of view, they don't maintain the same sort of momentum in material matters or professional situations. Keep it light and simple, that's the recipe for success this Wednesday. Since you are quite lucky under present trends, what about a shopping expedition?

18 THURSDAY   *Moon Age Day 9   Moon Sign Aquarius*

There is little reason why your plans should fail to materialise more or less the way you have envisaged them. There may be hurdles to overcome, but these are meat and drink to your zodiac sign at the present time. Some slight ill health is indicated for some Arians, though almost certainly of a very minor nature. Wrap up warm if it's cold though!

19 FRIDAY   *Moon Age Day 10   Moon Sign Aquarius*

It appears that your opinions carry a great deal of weight in the minds of your friends and colleagues. This is a time to show your ingenious nature working at its best. Socially speaking, you can enjoy a fairly easy-going sort of period and may not wish to be involved in lengthy or deep conversations of any sort.

20 SATURDAY *Moon Age Day 11 Moon Sign Pisces*

You should be making the most of all social encounters today, particularly ones that have shades of work associated with them. However, trying to think of something different to say to superiors can be a slight difficulty, especially if they are people for whom you have no real personal respect. Make sure you maintain a professional attitude at all times.

21 SUNDAY *Moon Age Day 12 Moon Sign Pisces*

If there is any way in which you can spoil yourself, today it is important that you utilise it. Of course you will not forget the responsibility you feel towards others but you can't be on duty all the time. It is important to sort out finances now, particularly those you share with other people.

22 MONDAY *Moon Age Day 13 Moon Sign Pisces*

If you box clever and use a little friendly persuasion today, especially at home, you can get people to do more or less whatever you wish. Some slight difficulties could be forthcoming with younger family members but this is really only a case of trying to see things from their point of view.

23 TUESDAY *Moon Age Day 14 Moon Sign Aries*

There is now room to grow and to think up interesting new ideas that are going to be extremely useful as this year comes to an end. Mental stimulus coming in from a number of different directions helps to push you forward at this time. Don't be too quick to judge the actions of a relative or a very close friend.

24 WEDNESDAY *Moon Age Day 15 Moon Sign Aries*

Things are hotting up again and the presence of the lunar high certainly helps you get ahead. You are now dynamic and raring to have a go at things that you shied away from only a day or two ago. If you want an October day on which it proves possible to move mountains, this could be it.

25 THURSDAY   *Moon Age Day 16   Moon Sign Taurus*

You might find it inspiring to seek out new contacts today, as well as getting a great deal from people who figure prominently in your life. Personal relationships should also be looking good and you have more than a slight chance of getting ahead of the game in the financial stakes.

26 FRIDAY   *Moon Age Day 17   Moon Sign Taurus*

Having moved steadily towards some of your life's goals in the recent past, you now find yourself at some sort of culmination point. That means looking again at issues and deciding where your effort is best concentrated henceforth. A chat with your partner or family members could help.

27 SATURDAY   *Moon Age Day 18   Moon Sign Gemini*

You might be kept in the dark regarding the plan of action that others are laying. It really is up to you to make certain that you are not ignored and that your point of view gets an airing. If this means being even nosier than usual, then so be it. There is also a chance of new personalities entering your life around now.

28 SUNDAY   *Moon Age Day 19   Moon Sign Gemini*

This is an excellent time to broaden your horizons in a general sense but you could also find yourself making a journey to a place of interest. Certainly, finding yourself stuck in any sort of rut has no appeal for you whatsoever. Those Arians who can take a break now are the luckiest of all; even a Sunday drive or walk would be beneficial.

29 MONDAY   *Moon Age Day 20   Moon Sign Cancer*

It is possible that the working week begins with you thinking of number one. As an Aries, you know that this can be a little weakness of yours, especially when it leads you to disregard the feelings of others. Keep in mind today that the planets are bringing this tendency to the fore and take especial care to avoid any negative situations arising from it.

30 TUESDAY · Moon Age Day 21 · Moon Sign Cancer

A fun and sociable sort of day is on the cards. You can expect to benefit from some help and support from people around you, even those you don't know very well. This will lighten the load of responsibility and enable you to focus on the good times. Make sure you say 'thank you' though!

31 WEDNESDAY · Moon Age Day 22 · Moon Sign Cancer

In the hustle and bustle of a busy working week, you might fail to notice what is going on at home. That could turn out to be something of a mistake, so find a few moments to check out the feelings of loved ones, especially your partner. Living in a world that only includes you would definitely be a mistake at this time.

November

2018

1 THURSDAY
Moon Age Day 23   Moon Sign Leo

Although some goals and ambitions seem a long way off, with a little patience you can start an important personal journey today. In terms of your career, a plan of action may fail to yield the sort of results you would wish. Don't abandon what you have thought up but rather look at things afresh and make some modifications.

2 FRIDAY
Moon Age Day 24   Moon Sign Leo

Working slowly but definitely towards your objectives you ought to be fired up with enthusiasm and quite happy to ring the changes socially. It is at work that the greatest movement begins to show and this continues until the weekend. Significant progress is possible, at least for a day or two.

3 SATURDAY
Moon Age Day 25   Moon Sign Virgo

You have a strong desire to be in the know at the moment and a need to be aware of how and why things work in the way they do. There is much about today that will fascinate you. When it comes to social encounters you are the centre of attraction and can get other people on your side when it proves to be necessary.

4 SUNDAY
Moon Age Day 26   Moon Sign Virgo

There is assistance around if you need it but in the main you are happy to go your own way and won't be held back by insignificant details. Absolute determination is the key to Aries success at present. Today looks as though it will bring plenty of energy and a great deal of determination to get ahead in any way you can.

5 MONDAY
Moon Age Day 27   Moon Sign Libra

Avoid signing documents or making agreements today unless you have read the small print very carefully and be particularly scrupulous in all business dealings. The lunar low could make your professional successes fairly minimal, and yet this is a time during which personal attachments can offer a great deal.

6 TUESDAY
Moon Age Day 28   Moon Sign Libra

In all probability those around you definitely do have your best interests at heart and so calling upon them for any sort of assistance won't be a problem. Romance is also well starred under present trends. It is clear that you are now keen to seek out new horizons and to do what appeals in an adventurous sense.

7 WEDNESDAY
Moon Age Day 0   Moon Sign Scorpio

Following the lunar low this could prove to be one of the best days of November when it comes to career interests. However, do take care to diversify when necessary and don't allow yourself to get stuck in any sort of rut. Listen to some sound professional advice from someone in the know.

8 THURSDAY
Moon Age Day 1   Moon Sign Scorpio

In all probability this will not be the best time for keeping up a high social profile. Although it isn't a common occurrence for you, there is a tendency for you to be quite shy today. Deal with this very temporary phase by concentrating on those things you know to be of importance and leave the social niceties until later.

9 FRIDAY
Moon Age Day 2   Moon Sign Sagittarius

At work you need to show a very positive face to new incentives, even if you have doubts about them. News from far off should prove to be a good stimulus to your personal life. Maybe someone you haven't heard from for ages is getting in touch again, offering you a journey or the chance to plan one.

10 SATURDAY   *Moon Age Day 3   Moon Sign Sagittarius*

Arians who take a responsible attitude to life will already be planning for Christmas and today would be fine for shopping or for looking carefully at exactly what is available to spend. You may be too busy to think much about money in a day-to-day sense and yet it is very important to do so.

11 SUNDAY   *Moon Age Day 4   Moon Sign Sagittarius*

Creature comforts have slightly less appeal now and you are willing to go without almost anything in the search to get what you really want from life. This would be another favourable time to broaden your horizons, though you probably won't begin doing so until the middle of the day.

12 MONDAY   *Moon Age Day 5   Moon Sign Capricorn*

Loving relationships are quite obvious as a place to go once the working day is over, but trends suggest that the comfort you find there might be marred by certain family members behaving in a less than typical way. Don't allow this to spoil your pleasure in your downtime, as tomorrow you will need to work hard once again.

13 TUESDAY   *Moon Age Day 6   Moon Sign Capricorn*

Today brings a great sense of wonder and a desire to consider all the options, making this a rather special, if somewhat odd, day. As you embark on your personal voyage of discovery, don't be at all surprised if you discover some facts and figures that give you a greater understanding of the way the world works.

14 WEDNESDAY   *Moon Age Day 7   Moon Sign Aquarius*

The active and enterprising side of your nature is on display, at least in a planning sense as, in fact, the activity has to come later. You may not be exactly moving any mountains but you can enjoy yourself in a quiet way and perhaps get to know someone close to you better than has been the case for quite a while.

15 THURSDAY   *Moon Age Day 8   Moon Sign Aquarius*

Concentrate on the matter at hand today, even though trends suggest that this might be quite difficult. When the practicalities are out of the way, make the most of very favourable social and romantic trends. This is an ideal time to decide whether you should jettison some aspects of life that are now of little or no use to you.

16 FRIDAY   *Moon Age Day 9   Moon Sign Aquarius*

Social and teamwork matters are favourably highlighted now, leading to a feeling that you can get on well with just about anyone. Perhaps you are slightly more considerate regarding the feelings of those around you than you are sometimes inclined to be. Take note of the positive reaction that comes from this and store it away for times when you default to a less empathetic frame of mind.

17 SATURDAY   ☿   *Moon Age Day 10   Moon Sign Pisces*

While your ability to concentrate on detailed work could be lacking today, you can make up for this with your enthusiasm for social events, especially if you don't work at the weekend. Don't stress if you can't achieve everything you set out to do but focus on the good mood that the present fun-loving Aries is enjoying.

18 SUNDAY   ☿   *Moon Age Day 11   Moon Sign Pisces*

Trends suggest that right now you are getting your own way in almost everything. It should prove easy to achieve your personal goals and you are drawing closer and closer to a time when you can ease off some of the pressure and gain from the work you put in before. That's not the case yet – but you still have rather a good day in store.

19 MONDAY   ☿   *Moon Age Day 12   Moon Sign Aries*

You start today on a mental and physical peak and won't have very much trouble at all letting others know that you mean business. So good is the impression you are giving that you might be offered some new opportunities. Nobody could fail to register your very positive presence at this stage of the month.

20 TUESDAY ☿ *Moon Age Day 13* *Moon Sign Aries*

The lunar high can set this part of the working week apart, though you will have to put in some effort yourself. If people are reluctant to go along with your plans, try talking them into co-operating. There is very little around to prevent you from getting what you want just now, either personally or professionally.

21 WEDNESDAY ☿ *Moon Age Day 14* *Moon Sign Taurus*

Don't become dominated by negative behavioural patterns. Stick to what you're good at, stay cheerful and make as many jokes as you can. That's the way most people like you to be and it can get you a long way. Conforming to expectations at work might be the most difficult job of all.

22 THURSDAY ☿ *Moon Age Day 15* *Moon Sign Taurus*

Prepare for a fairly average sort of day and don't push your luck too much. It won't be long before you are back on top form again but just for now you have little choice but to settle for second best. Conforming to the expectations that friends have of you could seem tedious but it does help your overall reputation.

23 FRIDAY ☿ *Moon Age Day 16* *Moon Sign Taurus*

Pleasure seeking and self-indulgence appear to be the order of the day. This is fine, but there will come a time when you feel in need of a little introspection. Mixing and mingling the possibilities of this day is what makes it uniquely interesting, but put off tedious jobs that bore you for another day if you can.

24 SATURDAY ☿ *Moon Age Day 17* *Moon Sign Gemini*

Some emotions are very close to the surface at present, particularly at home. This means that you could be rather touchier than would normally be the case. Try to find ways today to enjoy yourself and put some of your responsibilities on the back burner. Trends suggest that family members should be doing their best to be accommodating.

25 SUNDAY ☿ *Moon Age Day 18 Moon Sign Gemini*

Professional objectives need to be handled especially carefully right now. If you are at work today there are possible defeats in view, and you won't take kindly to this at all. Think before you act and if you are in any doubt, don't act at all. If you are not at work, take any chance to be involved in social gatherings that require little from you except your presence.

26 MONDAY ☿ *Moon Age Day 19 Moon Sign Cancer*

It is easy to tell today how many people hold you in high esteem. You could be surprised at the number, particularly if you learn you are popular with a few people you didn't think liked you at all. Don't be slow when it comes to asking for what you want, especially in a material sense.

27 TUESDAY ☿ *Moon Age Day 20 Moon Sign Cancer*

This should prove to be an industrious period, though there might not be much time for enjoyment. Aries is on full alert now and making the most of every opportunity that comes along. But how important is that if you don't manage to have some fun along the way? Balance in everything is the key.

28 WEDNESDAY ☿ *Moon Age Day 21 Moon Sign Leo*

Matters close to your heart are boosted today and that sensitivity, so much on display recently, is now stronger than ever. Not all your wishes come true right now but you should be willing to put in that extra bit of personal effort that will make all the difference. The world might struggle to keep up with you today.

29 THURSDAY ☿ *Moon Age Day 22 Moon Sign Leo*

Your love life should be highly rewarding today so expect some lovely romantic moments. This positive mood makes for another excellent period in this sphere of your life. Generally, you seem to be enjoying a high level of popularity, with people virtually lining up to help you out in any way they can.

30 FRIDAY ☿ *Moon Age Day 23 Moon Sign Virgo*

In terms of progress towards major ambitions this is likely to be a fairly quiet sort of day. That's good, because it means you can concentrate on having fun, in the company of people you care for a great deal. Beware of possible deception, perhaps coming from the direction of someone you once called a friend.

December

2018

1 SATURDAY ☿ *Moon Age Day 24 Moon Sign Virgo*

Aries is extremely innovative at the moment and others would be sensible if they took notice of what you have to say. Friends should be especially attentive. You make your way in life by relying on your own ideas and your ability to think up new concepts – and nothing is different about that situation now.

2 SUNDAY ☿ *Moon Age Day 25 Moon Sign Libra*

If you want a day during which you can make an impact on the world, this is not it. Instead of trying to do everything yourself, allow others to take at least part of the strain. This does not mean you are likely to lose control, so don't get upset about a fairly compulsory layoff that only lasts a couple of days.

3 MONDAY ☿ *Moon Age Day 26 Moon Sign Libra*

Not everyone is going to behave as you might have imagined and you will need some flexibility to cope with this. A charming social performance on your part could impress any number of people. Astrological trends point to a rather unusual start to the week and a time during which you could easily be surprised.

4 TUESDAY ☿ *Moon Age Day 27 Moon Sign Scorpio*

Almost anyone will be pleased to hear what you have to say right now and their reactions could be surprising. All aspects of communication are going extremely well at present. With some entertaining people on the horizon and almost everything going your way, the time has come to put your thoughts into tangible form.

5 WEDNESDAY ☿ *Moon Age Day 28 Moon Sign Scorpio*

Routine is something you would not welcome right now and it is quite obvious that you are up for as much variety in life as you can get. Your energy levels are now plentiful and you will have little or no difficulty in getting what you need from life, even if you cannot manage to get everything you want.

6 THURSDAY ☿ *Moon Age Day 29 Moon Sign Scorpio*

Confidence remains the key and the world marvels at your versatility. Communications work favourably now in order to bring you what you want the most. There may also be a slightly inward-looking tendency developing so that it isn't so much a matter of what you can achieve that counts but rather why.

7 FRIDAY *Moon Age Day 0 Moon Sign Sagittarius*

There is much activity today and, perhaps, a desire to get as much Christmas shopping done as early as you can. Intellectual stimulus is what you really need and you will deliberately be offering yourself up for puzzles of one sort or another. These could be practical in nature or simply for the sake of entertainment.

8 SATURDAY *Moon Age Day 1 Moon Sign Sagittarius*

After a really hectic week you might decide that it's time to simply have some fun and nobody is going to argue with that. Avoid getting involved in a domestic dustup and instead show that you are sweetness and light to everyone. In group or co-operative matters you make certain you are on the winning side.

9 SUNDAY *Moon Age Day 2 Moon Sign Capricorn*

A change of pace would do you the world of good around now. Leave work issues on the back burner for Sunday at least and concentrate instead on what your social life is presently offering. This may not be the best time of all for starting a new health regime but in the end only you can be the judge.

10 MONDAY   *Moon Age Day 3   Moon Sign Capricorn*

Socially speaking you appear to be on top form and will even be forging alliances with people you haven't necessarily seen eye to eye with in the past. The attitudes and opinions of family members may be quite surprising at times. The opportunity for meeting new people has rarely been better than it is right now.

11 TUESDAY   *Moon Age Day 4   Moon Sign Aquarius*

You have masses of energy and will be able to operate on several different fronts at the same time. There are significant gains in the offing and a chance to show your mettle at exactly the right time. There is something of the warrior about you at the moment and it is very unlikely that you would be settling for second best.

12 WEDNESDAY   *Moon Age Day 5   Moon Sign Aquarius*

Though you may not enjoy quite as much progress as you would wish in the practical world, getting along with others has rarely been easier. With the lunar high not all that far away, you can use present trends to set up meetings for next week. Once work is out of the way, find different ways in which to enjoy yourself.

13 THURSDAY   *Moon Age Day 6   Moon Sign Aquarius*

You should be feeling fairly good about yourself today and it is clear that you are taking a more dominant role at this stage of December. This will be especially true in any sort of family arrangements. Stand by for a crackerjack of a time ahead and one that offers much in the way of change.

14 FRIDAY   *Moon Age Day 7   Moon Sign Pisces*

A period of potential financial improvement is at hand. This is obviously a positive thing so close to Christmas. Part of the situation depends upon you looking carefully at your own money, and seeing how you can rationalise some spending. In the end you should find yourself better off than you thought.

15 SATURDAY   *Moon Age Day 8   Moon Sign Pisces*

The emphasis you wish to place on material and professional plans now receives a very definite boost. Make an early start and you should find you get on top of things quickly. Routines are definitely out at present as you move forward positively into areas of life that fascinate you.

16 SUNDAY   *Moon Age Day 9   Moon Sign Pisces*

The more settled amongst you will be consolidating personal attachments and finding moments to say those little words that are most important. Family-motivated interests probably dominate as Christmas approaches. Trends also suggest that a social contact could develop into something much more if you are an Aries who is open to new romance.

17 MONDAY   *Moon Age Day 10   Moon Sign Aries*

New avenues of communication tend to open up during this, the most potentially interesting of times. Although it might sometimes be further to the winning post that you might have imagined, it's worth keeping on running in almost any situation. Success can be truly yours with only a modicum of effort now.

18 TUESDAY   *Moon Age Day 11   Moon Sign Aries*

There is more than a small element of luck attending anything you undertake now and the lunar high helps you in other ways too. Romance is high on your agenda and some Arians will notice that potential affection is not only coming from expected directions. You are simply very attractive at present.

19 WEDNESDAY   *Moon Age Day 12   Moon Sign Taurus*

Don't be surprised if certain career issues and opportunities make themselves known at this stage of the week, immediately ahead of the Christmas break. There isn't much you can do about them now and by the middle of the day your thought will almost certainly have turned in a less practical and a more seasonal direction.

20 THURSDAY   *Moon Age Day 13   Moon Sign Taurus*

Social meetings and talks of various kinds should be highly rewarding. There is much good humour about and with Christmas just around the corner, it's clear that you are out to enjoy yourself as much as you can. Don't overtax your mind in terms of practical matters – today you need to party.

21 FRIDAY   *Moon Age Day 14   Moon Sign Gemini*

The trends around now are slightly unhelpful when it comes to general communication. If someone seems rather critical of either your attitude or approach, simply ignore what they have to say and get on with your own life. There is no point in reacting to situations you can't alter. A cheerful attitude is everything today.

22 SATURDAY   *Moon Age Day 15   Moon Sign Gemini*

It may not be quite as simple to get through to people today as you might have expected. It doesn't matter if you have to explain yourself two, or even three times. What remains important is to ensure that those closest to you understand perfectly what you are trying to tell them. For once you show supreme patience.

23 SUNDAY   *Moon Age Day 16   Moon Sign Cancer*

Test your luck today because it is highly unlikely to let you down. Routines could be something of a bind, so avoid them altogether if you possibly can. Meanwhile you push forward progressively and will already have begun the round of parties and enjoyment that means Christmas to you.

24 MONDAY   *Moon Age Day 17   Moon Sign Cancer*

A romantic offer could be coming your way, particularly if you have been searching for new beginnings. Your confidence is generally high at the moment though you will have your work cut out keeping all the balls in the air that you are juggling right now. Don't forget, Christmas is only a day away.

25 TUESDAY
Moon Age Day 18   Moon Sign Leo

On Christmas Day the planets are working well for you, a fact that brings a high degree of warmth to the festivities as far as you are concerned. Close attachments are the most memorable at this time, whilst getting on side with younger people turns out to be much easier than you thought. A happy and satisfying day is in prospect.

26 WEDNESDAY
Moon Age Day 19   Moon Sign Leo

Boxing Day could be a great time for gathering new information, as well as for interpreting the facts and figures of life in quite a new way. You won't be unduly stressed at present, though one or two family members could be. Try to offer the help you can and provide a listening ear.

27 THURSDAY
Moon Age Day 20   Moon Sign Virgo

There is likely to be a great deal of coming and going today, so much so that you might find it difficult to actually concentrate on anything at all. Maybe that's no bad thing. Specifics are not what your life is about right now and a little guesswork is part of the present Aries way to success.

28 FRIDAY
Moon Age Day 21   Moon Sign Virgo

Stand by for an advantageous period financially and to discover a new way to build up your personal fortune. This looks likely to develop over the weeks and months ahead but the process begins now. You strike a good balance between spending and saving, together with some important new ideas that are going to work well for you.

29 SATURDAY
Moon Age Day 22   Moon Sign Libra

Those around you might be surprised at your tendency to avoid too much alcohol or rich food. Still, you will be content and happy with your lot and in a position to offer much support to family members and friends. Trends suggest that you may not feel any particular drive to push yourself forward or to live the high life.

30 SUNDAY
Moon Age Day 23   Moon Sign Libra

If you feel rather out of sorts right now, blame the fact that the Moon is in your opposite zodiac sign. At least you get this interlude out of the way before the New Year celebrations and generally have positive influences ahead of you for the remainder of the month. All that is required at the moment is some patience.

31 MONDAY
Moon Age Day 24   Moon Sign Libra

Any resolutions for the year ahead could include a determination to push your practical capabilities to the full. You will want to be noticed today as the lunar low fades and should go to great lengths to make sure that you are not ignored by anyone. Beware of alienating others by adopting an attitude they cannot understand.

ARIES:
2019 DIARY PAGES

ARIES:
YOUR YEAR IN BRIEF

Almost from the very start of the year it should be obvious that you are keen to get on with things and that you will be putting behind you some of the less favourable aspects of 2018. In January and February you could be going through a time of retrenchment. You will be anxious to make progress at work but may have slightly less time for relatives and friends as a result. Your confidence should be especially high as February comes to an end.

March and April should bring you to a better understanding of what is necessary if you want to make real progress in your life this year. As time goes by your confidence should grow, especially as you receive tangible support from people who are in the best position to offer it. Money matters should strengthen and there is a good chance of travel, especially during April. What you bring back may be of some importance.

Now things begin to get interesting. May and June bring you closer to your heart's desire as you wake up to the possibilities that surround you. During May you will be pleased to travel more and should also be on the receiving end of social invitations that could, in the longer-term, revolutionise your life. Don't give in to any emotional blackmail, stick to your guns.

The high summer has much to offer you. July and August reverberate with new opportunities and you grab them with both hands. A tedious and long-lasting job will probably be completed now and you have it within your power to help a friend who is desperately in need of your support. You prove just how reliable you are but at the same time you retain the degree of flexibility that is indicative of your zodiac sign.

During September and October you recognise your own capability. At this time you are likely to discover skills you didn't know you possessed and your abilities will certainly impress other people. Personal attachments mean more to you at this stage of the year and some Arians could be finding new love under October's autumn star.

The final months of the year, November and December, might begin routinely but are unlikely to end that way. Now you are back to a time of year that suits you and you thrive when others shiver. Christmas should be especially rewarding and happy, bringing many genuine surprises and the chance to renew an old acquaintance or friendship. Make the most of New Year celebrations in order to make resolutions stick from the start.

January 2019

1 TUESDAY
Moon Age Day 25   Moon Sign Scorpio

You are not lacking in confidence as the new year begins and behave much more like your usual Arian self. Even though it's a bank holiday, there are gains to be made, particularly in a financial sense, and you might find quite a few people in your vicinity who reveal themselves to be both sensible and helpful. Look at new tasks as carefully as possible.

2 WEDNESDAY
Moon Age Day 26   Moon Sign Scorpio

The idea of taking up a new hobby may be appealing now, especially since the winter weather means you cannot get out and about as much as you might wish. Creatively speaking you are on top form, so you have nothing to lose. Don't be put off if small unforced errors creep into some of your efforts.

3 THURSDAY
Moon Age Day 27   Moon Sign Sagittarius

Rules and regulations are not always easy to follow now and you will tend to kick against at least some of them, especially if you know them to be plainly ridiculous. By all means work hard to stay ahead in certain respects but don't keep driving forward simply for the sake of doing so.

4 FRIDAY
Moon Age Day 28   Moon Sign Sagittarius

You are keen to enjoy whatever life has to offer now, which might be a great deal. Socially speaking life is likely to be very good and you have few worries to hold you back. There is just a small chance that personal relationships are not everything they might be so prepare for this and put in some extra effort.

5 SATURDAY　　*Moon Age Day 0　Moon Sign Capricorn*

At the start of today there seems to be tons to get done and very little time in which to do it. If anyone can manage this situation, Aries can. Don't allow yourself to be restricted by colleagues who have doubts about your reasoning. The sort of jobs you are undertaking at the moment can only be resolved on the hoof.

6 SUNDAY　　*Moon Age Day 1　Moon Sign Capricorn*

Your confidence is steady, but won't have been helped by a number of doubts that are circulating at present. There could be feelings of apprehension, or an inclination to see problems in front of you. A naturally suspicious mind is not usually your way so dismiss it out of hand.

7 MONDAY　　*Moon Age Day 2　Moon Sign Capricorn*

It appears that fun and games are the order of the day, mainly because you are in such a happy and positive frame of mind. Even people who often irritate you are less likely to cause you any concern today and you should also be able to deal with issues that have been of some concern recently.

8 TUESDAY　　*Moon Age Day 3　Moon Sign Aquarius*

In sporting activities, your naturally competitive nature is stepped up a gear. It's a fact that you don't like to lose at anything, and under current trends your desire to win may even tempt you to bend the rules somewhat. In matters of the heart you show yourself to be kind, sincere and extremely attentive.

9 WEDNESDAY　　*Moon Age Day 4　Moon Sign Aquarius*

You may experience some slight annoyance today if people don't do what they have promised. Getting to where you want to be might not be quite as easy without the support that was promised to you and this could lead to the odd spat, especially at work. Socially speaking, you exhibit far more patience.

10 THURSDAY
Moon Age Day 5   Moon Sign Pisces

Standing up for others is part of what this Thursday is about. Brave and even a little foolhardy, you take on some of the bullies in life that others leave alone. Aries is a natural street fighter, though fortunately only generally in a verbal sense. What you won't stand for today is any nonsense.

11 FRIDAY
Moon Age Day 6   Moon Sign Pisces

Trends suggest that anything really unusual will catch your interest now and may lead to some kind of personal investigation. It is also likely that part of your mind will be inclined to dwell in the past and you will find yourself looking back as much as forward. This is unlike Aries but it should turn out to be a very temporary trend.

12 SATURDAY
Moon Age Day 7   Moon Sign Pisces

Saturday should bring a break from the everyday routines of the week and could turn out to be a great day for shopping. From a financial point of view it is possible that you find yourself very slightly better off than you expected. If there are documents to be signed at present, take care to read the small print.

13 SUNDAY
Moon Age Day 8   Moon Sign Aries

Stand by for a very positive sort of Sunday. The Moon is back in your zodiac sign, bringing with it the lunar high, which means there is no likelihood of anyone failing to notice you tonight, no matter how you choose to spend your time. Aries is bang on form and everyone is going to know it. Keep your plans realistic, though.

14 MONDAY
Moon Age Day 9   Moon Sign Aries

The new week finds you anxious to have fun. The humorous side of your nature is in evidence and although you might tend to burn the candle at both ends today, people born under your zodiac sign can get away with doing so. Bear in mind that there will be some tasks that benefit from being left alone and looked at again later.

15 TUESDAY   *Moon Age Day 10   Moon Sign Taurus*

Today you feel the need to communicate with influential people and if you heed this advice, you could reap further rewards as the month advances. You may not have life all your own way but in a romantic sense things are likely to work out well. There are distinct advantages to the way Aries looks at life right now.

16 WEDNESDAY   *Moon Age Day 11   Moon Sign Taurus*

This is a good time to be taking calculated risks, especially at work. Of course you won't want to put your safety on the line but the odd chance when it comes to your contact with superiors or those in a position of influence could work out well. Your confidence in your ability to say and do the right thing remains essentially strong.

17 THURSDAY   *Moon Age Day 12   Moon Sign Taurus*

There is a lot of energy behind almost everything you either think or say today. Although this isn't unusual for Aries your efforts are more concentrated and effective than ever right now. It is important to be selective in your choices if you want to make the very best impression on the world at large.

18 FRIDAY   *Moon Age Day 13   Moon Sign Gemini*

Focus on finances today and try to work out some sort of cohesive plan for the future. You might be slightly luckier than of late and will certainly have what it takes to see the bigger picture. Friends are likely to be very supportive and might also find you particularly attractive now.

19 SATURDAY   *Moon Age Day 14   Moon Sign Gemini*

This looks likely to be a good period in terms of finances and a time during which you can consolidate your position and perhaps even move forward somewhat. This hasn't necessarily been the case over the last few months so you should find that you are feeling rather more secure in the weeks that lie ahead.

20 SUNDAY — *Moon Age Day 15   Moon Sign Cancer*

You may receive a gift of appreciation from someone who has a very good reason to thank you for your efforts on their behalf. A change of scenery would do you a great deal of good at the moment because although it is still the middle of the winter, you are restless and in need of some amusement.

21 MONDAY — *Moon Age Day 16   Moon Sign Cancer*

Now is a period for gathering information and for looking ahead to a time when you will be somehow freer than appears to be the case now. Although instilling patience into your nature is never easy, it is especially required at the moment. Don't get on the wrong side of the very people who can help you the most.

22 TUESDAY — *Moon Age Day 17   Moon Sign Leo*

You desire freedom at almost any cost and that can lead you into a little trouble at times. It would be better if you looked ahead carefully but this is the last thing you are likely to be doing right now. People you don't see often might be the ones to offer you the soundest advice and it would be sensible to at least listen to them.

23 WEDNESDAY — *Moon Age Day 18   Moon Sign Leo*

There are gains to be made now although these are more positively highlighted in your professional life than your personal life. At the same time you could find yourself to be quite restless and inclined to make demands of yourself rather than others. Arians always have a tendency to become a little touchy if they are not happy with their own progress.

24 THURSDAY — *Moon Age Day 19   Moon Sign Virgo*

Social trends should be working out nicely and there isn't much doubt that you wear your charm like a glove. When Aries is on good form, everyone can be happy. In any sort of party setting you really shine at present and there is no doubt at all that you will be attracting more than a few admirers.

25 FRIDAY
Moon Age Day 20   Moon Sign Virgo

Your vitality and sense of optimism are strong and as a result you show the very best qualities of your zodiac sign to the world at large. Everyone loves you and that makes you happy because you really do wish to be popular. The present astrological trends favour adventures or educational endeavours of almost any sort.

26 SATURDAY
Moon Age Day 21   Moon Sign Libra

Today may find you feeling slightly under par. The lunar low will be around for the weekend, which could make it difficult to react to matters immediately or to be as inspirational as you would wish. Stick to family relationships wherever possible and enjoy a stay-at-home sort of day.

27 SUNDAY
Moon Age Day 22   Moon Sign Libra

This particular Sunday may prove to be less rewarding than you might have hoped. You have to get used to the fact that the Moon in Libra is going to slow you down somewhat. However, once you realise that this means you have the chance to relax, this planetary situation takes on a different dimension.

28 MONDAY
Moon Age Day 23   Moon Sign Scorpio

Don't do too much dreaming today. Finding the right balance between thoughts and actions is certainly not easy at the moment but when life is too simple you become bored. There may be some entertaining opportunities on offer, but if they are not forthcoming you are quick to make up your own adventure.

29 TUESDAY
Moon Age Day 24   Moon Sign Scorpio

Don't be in too much of a rush to achieve all your material objectives if only because you will need to save some activities for later. Spend a few hours enjoying what is around you now and mix as freely as you can with relatives and friends alike. For a few hours you can afford to genuinely relax.

30 WEDNESDAY *Moon Age Day 25   Moon Sign Sagittarius*

This is a good time for social groups and for getting to grips with issues that have been waiting around for some time. Your confidence grows significantly as you realise that much of your effort towards the end of last year is now beginning to pay dividends. Routines can be boring so change them if you can.

31 THURSDAY *Moon Age Day 26   Moon Sign Sagittarius*

There is plenty to keep you fairly happy and busily on the go today. All the same, it's important to organise your personal schedule as carefully as you can to avoid confusion in certain issues. Trends suggest that some Arians may be a little absentminded today, so make a note of important information.

February
2019

1 FRIDAY
Moon Age Day 27   Moon Sign Sagittarius

There really is no need to rush things at work today so avoid this tendency and you will put yourself in a good position to achieve firm, sensible results. Colleagues and friends alike should prove to be very helpful and might also come up with some ideas to complement those you are having at present.

2 SATURDAY
Moon Age Day 28   Moon Sign Capricorn

You may meet people now who have the ability to broaden your own perspectives. All in all this should be a fairly productive sort of day, with possibly a little adventure thrown in for good measure. A fly in the ointment could come from a friend who is clearly in need of more than a little emotional support.

3 SUNDAY
Moon Age Day 29   Moon Sign Capricorn

In a social sense, Aries has a thirst for freedom and new experiences during much of today. Just following paths you know to have been made for you won't be of much interest because the pioneering spirit within you is strong. You may arrive at some quite startling conclusions regarding a friend.

4 MONDAY
Moon Age Day 0   Moon Sign Aquarius

You could enjoy considerable success at work at the start of this new week. Don't be too quick to put forward your point of view if you know it will clash with that of someone who has control over part of your life. It isn't your way to suck up to anyone but a little tact won't cost you much and could bring gains.

5 TUESDAY · *Moon Age Day 1 · Moon Sign Aquarius*

You positively shine in social situations and can be the life and soul of any party that is taking place in your vicinity right now. You are strong and confident and you certainly won't be lacking when it comes to making the most favourable impression imaginable. This could be a very fortunate day.

6 WEDNESDAY · *Moon Age Day 2 · Moon Sign Aquarius*

A financial matter may appear to put you under some pressure and careful thought is necessary if you are not to lose out in the money stakes. In a more personal matter, it is important to see things from the perspective of someone you love. While it might be difficult to adopt a different mindset, it is important.

7 THURSDAY · *Moon Age Day 3 · Moon Sign Pisces*

Both emotional and material affairs may improve today thanks to the intervention and advice of a loved one. Mental endeavours are also especially favoured and communication with others is the key to greater personal success. The fact that you will be in demand does absolutely nothing to slow you down.

8 FRIDAY · *Moon Age Day 4 · Moon Sign Pisces*

Your intuition regarding the behaviour and thought processes of others is very strong today and certainly should not be ignored. You are also very forthright when it comes to expressing your opinions, so much so that you can turn a few heads. Maybe a little less reaction and a greater degree of understanding is called for.

9 SATURDAY · *Moon Age Day 5 · Moon Sign Aries*

You won't need a second chance today if you get the opportunity to pull off a significant coup. The lunar high offers you incentive and initiative in abundance, bringing one of the most progressive days during the whole of February. More than a little good luck attends your efforts, too.

10 SUNDAY *Moon Age Day 6 Moon Sign Aries*

You have a great deal of vitality and also a desire to push through obstacles to get what you want from life. Aries may be a beacon of positivity and an inspiration to others at this time and you have the ability to help people without even really trying. There are gains coming from some surprising directions so keep your eyes open.

11 MONDAY *Moon Age Day 7 Moon Sign Aries*

Conversation and general communication are the keys to success at the start of this working week. Although you might think you are saying too much for your own good around now, this really isn't the case. Don't be afraid to put forward an alternative opinion, even when dealing with those who are in charge.

12 TUESDAY *Moon Age Day 8 Moon Sign Taurus*

Your present talent for analysis makes it easy for you to work out why others are behaving in the way they are. Casual conversations can lead you to some startling conclusions and may bring unexpected incentives. Trends suggest that there is something especially warm and inviting about romantic attachments now.

13 WEDNESDAY *Moon Age Day 9 Moon Sign Taurus*

This is a time when things definitely do go better in pairs. In business, or in romance, you are now happy to co-operate and to take someone else into your confidence. There are very few around you at present who could fail to fall under that magic Arian spell.

14 THURSDAY *Moon Age Day 10 Moon Sign Gemini*

Don't expect your opinions to go unchallenged by others today. As a rule, a great many people tend to defer to your judgement because you always appear to know what you are talking about. Unfortunately, this might not be the case now and so it is possible that you will have some explaining to do.

15 FRIDAY   *Moon Age Day 11   Moon Sign Gemini*

Positive trends continue and you may choose to focus more of your attention on romance. Whoever the target of your affection is at the moment, they are lucky indeed. Nobody can compliment like you right now and your words are more readily accepted because you make it plain that they are the truth.

16 SATURDAY   *Moon Age Day 12   Moon Sign Cancer*

A change of scenery does you good, as would meeting new people, or at least those you haven't seen for quite some time. Make the most of offers that come your way, especially social ones. Don't try to get through too much in a practical sense, even though you should feel physically fit.

17 SUNDAY   *Moon Age Day 13   Moon Sign Cancer*

This is a Sunday on which you can make good use of your time and energy. Planning ahead is important too, with the possibility of family meetings that will allow you to come to terms with the ideas of others. This time of year isn't your favourite but you can get ahead despite the cold weather and lack of sunshine.

18 MONDAY   *Moon Age Day 14   Moon Sign Leo*

Don't take on too many commitments in a short space of time today. You need moments to please yourself, and to make sure that your actions are sound. The more you do, the less likely you are to do any of it really well. One honest task, superbly crafted, is all that this day requires of you.

19 TUESDAY   *Moon Age Day 15   Moon Sign Leo*

You could be feeling unusually sensitive today. That's fine, but you can't expect those around you to be clairvoyant. They will treat you to the same verbal rough and tumble you usually enjoy. If you do find you are being teased, remember that what is being said comes with genuine affection.

20 WEDNESDAY *Moon Age Day 16   Moon Sign Virgo*

An ongoing period of contentment, especially with regard to romantic relationships, is indicated by present planetary trends. There is a sense that you are getting back from attachments what you have been willing to put into them up to now. Learning what others think of you can be a happy experience today.

21 THURSDAY *Moon Age Day 17   Moon Sign Virgo*

You may have a slight tendency to adopt a 'me first' attitude today. Aries is hardly the most retiring or least arrogant of the zodiac signs, but generally you do have a sort of regal humility that takes over when you are too puffed up. Look for it today and make certain you don't offer any inadvertent offence.

22 FRIDAY *Moon Age Day 18   Moon Sign Libra*

The smooth running of your life is less obvious now that the lunar low is here. For today and tomorrow it may be inevitable that you come across a number of obstacles. Don't be too willing to postpone an outing or a meeting just because you don't feel in the mood for it. Some extra effort may be required but it will pay dividends.

23 SATURDAY *Moon Age Day 19   Moon Sign Libra*

A little rest and relaxation is what the doctor ordered now. Although you kept pushing forward yesterday, it is much more likely you will simply put your feet up today. Try to avoid starting anything new for the moment and be willing instead to look at plans you are presently laying down for the medium-term future.

24 SUNDAY *Moon Age Day 20   Moon Sign Scorpio*

It's definitely a case of off with the old and on with the new now, on one of the most progressive Sundays that you have experienced so far this year. Not everyone around you is likely to be immediately willing to fall into line with what you think is best, but with a little persuasion and a good deal of charm you can win them round.

25 MONDAY *Moon Age Day 21   Moon Sign Scorpio*

New information gleaned from others can put you firmly in the picture as far as work is concerned, but it is possible that a few friends might adopt a rather strange attitude and will need you to counsel them carefully. Your own personal life now ought to be settled, with your partner or lover behaving pretty much as you would expect.

26 TUESDAY *Moon Age Day 22   Moon Sign Sagittarius*

Though minor obligations are inclined to get in your way today, in the main you are moving forward in a satisfactory manner. You could still feel somewhat restless and perhaps trapped by circumstance. The way out of this state of affairs is to simply keep busy and to ignore little worries.

27 WEDNESDAY *Moon Age Day 23   Moon Sign Sagittarius*

In a career sense, this can be a taxing time. The problem is that you are trying to get ahead but little frustrations and obligations keep holding you back. You are more than capable of dealing with such situations, particularly because your social and personal life is so settled at the moment.

28 THURSDAY *Moon Age Day 24   Moon Sign Sagittarius*

You now benefit from continued ease of movement through the various facets of your life. Perhaps the best area today is love, which you offer and receive in equal measure. Any task that has to be performed works best when you do it in co-operation with a loved one, or just maybe a trusted, long-time friend.

March

2019

1 FRIDAY
Moon Age Day 25   Moon Sign Capricorn

In the workplace you probably need a slightly higher degree of self-discipline than you are exhibiting at the moment. If you experience certain limitations you will need to concentrate solely on what you are doing. Friends can be helpful, though colleagues may prove less so for today.

2 SATURDAY
Moon Age Day 26   Moon Sign Capricorn

Your love of freedom grows by the hour and could display itself in the way you fight for others if you think they are being kept down in any way. Both intellectually and socially you want to make more of yourself and alongside this trend, the more adventurous side of Aries begins to reveal itself.

3 SUNDAY
Moon Age Day 27   Moon Sign Aquarius

When it comes to getting things done there is no doubt at all that you are showing your dynamic side now, and you will continue to do so for at least the next week or so. The time of year in which Aries wakes from its partial hibernation is coming around now and everyone is going to realise it.

4 MONDAY
Moon Age Day 28   Moon Sign Aquarius

Your mental and physical energies are focused, so much so that you might even be accused of being slightly aggressive. Although Aries is often quite sanguine, yours is after all a Fire sign, so your mood can be volatile on occasions. Reign in a tendency to spend money too liberally around now.

5 TUESDAY   *Moon Age Day 29   Moon Sign Aquarius*

Old situations have to be left where they belong today – in the past. You won't get very far if you are carrying around baggage from an earlier period. This is a time when you definitely need to look ahead, which is why nostalgia has very little part to play in your life between now and the early summer at least.

6 WEDNESDAY   ☿   *Moon Age Day 0   Moon Sign Pisces*

It is possible that some of your ideas and motives are being misinterpreted or simply not understood at all now. As a result it is important to explain yourself fully and to make absolutely certain that you haven't said the wrong thing by accident. One job at a time appears to be the rule of thumb now, which isn't always easy for Aries.

7 THURSDAY   ☿   *Moon Age Day 1   Moon Sign Pisces*

You have a superb talent for explaining yourself at the moment and are assisted in this by the changing position of the Moon. This will be a distinct advantage in making new social contacts and in coming to terms with a family issue that has been more or less ignored of late.

8 FRIDAY   ☿   *Moon Age Day 2   Moon Sign Aries*

Like pressing a button, all your energy and dynamism comes together today to offer a number of exciting new incentives. With plenty to work for and the lunar high supporting your efforts, this could be a rip-roaring day and one that offers more than enough excitement, even for an Arian.

9 SATURDAY   ☿   *Moon Age Day 3   Moon Sign Aries*

Important negotiations could be taking place today, even if you have to arrange them at fairly short notice. Go for gold in whatever you take on and expect to get what you want, especially at work. Trends also put the spotlight on Aries as a lover at the moment, so you should make time to think about romance once the practical matters are out of the way.

10 SUNDAY ☿ *Moon Age Day 4   Moon Sign Taurus*

An element of competition can be good for you, though there probably isn't that much place for it at the weekend unless you are taking part in sport. Certainly in a domestic sense what is required is co-operation. Prepare for the fact that keeping control of those more fiery qualities won't always be easy this weekend.

11 MONDAY ☿ *Moon Age Day 5   Moon Sign Taurus*

Many people will find you inspirational and will be only too happy to seek your company. Present planetary trends definitely motivate you to maintain good relations with the world at large and you demonstrate a fair and honest attitude in almost all circumstances. Trends also indicate that some strong personalities may cross your path around now.

12 TUESDAY ☿ *Moon Age Day 6   Moon Sign Taurus*

Romance has rarely been better starred in your chart than it is right now. A strong boost to your love life ought to be quite evident and Arians who have been looking for new relationships may find that their efforts have a greater chance of success. Finding what you want in a general sense ought to prove easy.

13 WEDNESDAY ☿ *Moon Age Day 7   Moon Sign Gemini*

Work and career developments may well take a fortunate turn today, so be prepared for the possibilities that could come along as a result. Use this period wisely and don't be tardy when it comes to speaking your mind even to someone you usually find a little intimidating. Act cautiously though, and always think through the consequences of your words.

14 THURSDAY ☿ *Moon Age Day 8   Moon Sign Gemini*

Along comes a period for travelling and for visiting interesting places. This trend applies not only to today but for several more to come, so your arrangements might involve the weekend ahead. Try to broaden your understanding of life, even if circumstances root you to the spot for now.

15 FRIDAY ☿ *Moon Age Day 9   Moon Sign Cancer*

There are planetary indications around now which suggest that Arians could become restless souls today, and may develop an insatiable appetite for new surroundings, situations and stimulus. Friends may be a help as some of them offer exactly what you are looking for. Don't be too quick to judge colleagues or you may find that you come unstuck later.

16 SATURDAY ☿ *Moon Age Day 10   Moon Sign Cancer*

Your potential for success is strong, and the only real stumbling block may be your ability to keep your friends working keenly on your behalf. Where practical and financial projects are concerned you are going to have to find some way to convince them that they are working towards their own betterment too.

17 SUNDAY ☿ *Moon Age Day 11   Moon Sign Cancer*

Mentally speaking, an intense view of life means you could so easily become obsessed with matters that are not really all that important. If you are suffering from some minor physical ailment, take a look at your working practices, which may hold the answer to the problem.

18 MONDAY ☿ *Moon Age Day 12   Moon Sign Leo*

Today you have the ability to charm those higher up the ladder of life to give you a hand up. Some Arians may be offered additional responsibilities at this time and are unlikely to turn down the opportunity. It may not be easy to conform to the expectations others have of you in a social sense, but you may need to if people are relying on you.

19 TUESDAY ☿ *Moon Age Day 13   Moon Sign Leo*

This is a time for getting down to the real nitty gritty of situations and for thinking them through very carefully indeed. Some conflict amongst your friends can be solved in minutes with your timely intervention, whilst romance looks better and stronger than for some days past.

20 WEDNESDAY ☿   *Moon Age Day 14*   *Moon Sign Virgo*

You seem to know instinctively today which elements of life you need to retain and which should be jettisoned. You are not in the least sentimental right now and would be quite willing to shove all manner of things in the dustbin. This doesn't simply include old furnishings, but a few redundant thoughts too.

21 THURSDAY ☿   *Moon Age Day 15*   *Moon Sign Virgo*

A matter connected with communication could run into trouble, perhaps because you are not quite as 'tuned in' as has been the case of late. You should also bear in mind that the Moon is fast approaching your opposite sign, which itself can lead to some confusion. Take particular care to explain yourself properly today.

22 FRIDAY ☿   *Moon Age Day 16*   *Moon Sign Libra*

Not everyone can be a winner on each and every day and it might be your turn on this one to feel like you are being put at the back of the queue. This isn't exactly true, but with the lunar low around at the moment, you are inclined to look on the negative side of any situation. Try to join in the fun that others are creating.

23 SATURDAY ☿   *Moon Age Day 17*   *Moon Sign Libra*

You may now feel the need to indulge some slightly selfish tendencies, which is often the resort of Aries if it feels it is being ignored. However, the difficulties created by the Moon in Libra will not persist and by the evening you should already be feeling more like your usual self.

24 SUNDAY ☿   *Moon Age Day 18*   *Moon Sign Scorpio*

You should be more or less back on course now and will notice that some of the problems of yesterday have now diminished, or perhaps disappeared altogether. Don't be too willing to listen to the advice of someone you have rarely trusted before. Your own decisions are the most important now.

25 MONDAY ☿ *Moon Age Day 19* *Moon Sign Scorpio*

Your need for personal freedom is likely to be emphasised above everything right now. As a principle this is fine, but there is a danger you could take things too far. Try to relax and to accept the benefits of whatever today has to offer. If you are obliged to work don't do any more than is strictly necessary.

26 TUESDAY ☿ *Moon Age Day 20* *Moon Sign Sagittarius*

Now is the time to get your foot down on the professional accelerator. You know what you want from life, and have a pretty good idea how you should go about getting it. There are details today that must not be left to chance so do not approach them with the hope that they will sort themselves out but take time to think them through properly.

27 WEDNESDAY ☿ *Moon Age Day 21* *Moon Sign Sagittarius*

Getting on with others might not be too easy just now. If you want to make certain that there are no hiccups in relationships today, stay close to those who know you well and who you can trust to be on your side. You may find that you begin to question some aspects of your social circle under present trends.

28 THURSDAY ☿ *Moon Age Day 22* *Moon Sign Capricorn*

You could find yourself in the right place at the right time to enjoy some financial benefits. This may be the product of some medium or long-term planning from the past that is finally maturing. Always think through any financial decisions carefully and seek independent advice before you act. Also, take care not to judge the actions of a friend without knowing the facts.

29 FRIDAY *Moon Age Day 23* *Moon Sign Capricorn*

Along comes a period when it seems vitally important to widen your horizons. It could be that you are only now waking up to the changing year and noticing that spring is in the air. In actual fact, though, the position of the Sun in your chart is the main culprit and it demands change of some sort.

30 SATURDAY   *Moon Age Day 24   Moon Sign Capricorn*

While some trends suggest that this is a good time for intellectual studies of any sort, others favour spending some time enjoying a little romance, too. Show your partner just how important they are to you and you may be surprised at the intensity of the response that comes back in your direction.

31 SUNDAY   *Moon Age Day 25   Moon Sign Aquarius*

You are clearly very anxious at the moment to push ahead with something important to you, but as this is a weekend make sure that you don't do this at the expense of enjoying some fun. There is a distinct possibility that you will get the urge to travel now, if not to exotic places, then at least to profitable ones.

April 2019

1 MONDAY
Moon Age Day 26   Moon Sign Aquarius

It is likely that your personal life will be more fulfilling now than might have been the case for quite some time. It also seems likely that you might choose to address your physical wellbeing. If you have decided to embark on a new diet or exercise regime, make sure that you take it steadily at first.

2 TUESDAY
Moon Age Day 27   Moon Sign Pisces

A wide rang of interests might appeal to you at the moment. This would certainly seem to be what the present planetary line-up is indicating, although unfortunately there are also certain tricky issues that are presently difficult to avoid. Turning your attention towards them won't be too appealing, but it could be necessary.

3 WEDNESDAY
Moon Age Day 28   Moon Sign Pisces

Intimate encounters with those you love today could put a different slant on issues that have been on your mind recently. Maybe you recognise that you have been taking things too seriously – or perhaps not seriously enough? Either way, there is food for thought and a slightly more serious Aries on view.

4 THURSDAY
Moon Age Day 29   Moon Sign Pisces

It is possible that you could lack a degree of patience with your partner or family members now and you may need to exercise a little self-discipline in this regard. Today can be good for all sorts of fun activities, especially if you are undertaking them alongside those who have the same desire to have a great time as you presently do.

5 FRIDAY
Moon Age Day 0   Moon Sign Aries

Today the Moon slips into the sign of Aries. As a result, you can expect a twofold sort of day. At first you may have some concerns about issues that seem to need attention, but by the afternoon all anxious thoughts are banished from your mind.

6 SATURDAY
Moon Age Day 1   Moon Sign Aries

Welcome to the bright time of the month. This Saturday ought to be a day when your own choices really count. There are plenty of people around to lend a hand, especially in a social sense. It is unlikely that you will be taking life too seriously but you still manage to score some successes all the same.

7 SUNDAY
Moon Age Day 2   Moon Sign Taurus

It appears that tomorrow you may get a chance to capitalise on the positive events of the last couple of days to make some financial gains. For today though, you are likely to be in a contemplative mood and quite happy to spend some time thinking things through. If someone in the family lets you down, there might be a sound reason for this.

8 MONDAY
Moon Age Day 3   Moon Sign Taurus

This is definitely a good time to let go and be yourself and refuse to be held back by anyone with a negative viewpoint. Try to engage people in the sort of conversation that suits you best, keeping the subject matter varied and interesting. But most important of all, stay away from controversy.

9 TUESDAY
Moon Age Day 4   Moon Sign Gemini

You seem to know how to get the best from relationships today, which is why you are spending so much time concentrating on them. In a more practical sense, don't be too willing to look at schemes that demand more of you than you are willing or able to give. You need to look at the future in a more specific and realistic way if you are to make progress.

10 WEDNESDAY · *Moon Age Day 5 · Moon Sign Gemini*

You are now looking towards the wider world in order to achieve the sense of purpose and fulfilment that is so important to the zodiac sign of Aries. It is highly unlikely that you will discover everything you need within your own personality or personal situations so you are right to think big, but remain realistic.

11 THURSDAY · *Moon Age Day 6 · Moon Sign Gemini*

Your career should now be running smoothly enough, which is why you tend to look around for something else with which you can tinker. The accent could fall upon friendship today but instead of trying to make your pals what you want them to be, look at their present problems and lend a hand.

12 FRIDAY · *Moon Age Day 7 · Moon Sign Cancer*

It would appear from prevailing planetary trends that almost the whole world is lining up to do you one favour or another. Don't turn away the help that is on offer, even when you are sure that you could do things better yourself. You need to be just as kind and tactful as possible today.

13 SATURDAY · *Moon Age Day 8 · Moon Sign Cancer*

Your creative potential is strong and this is almost certain to show in one way or another. You might feel the need to go off and do your own thing unrestricted by the practical necessities of life. A complete break from routine would do you the world of good if it is possible to arrange at such short notice.

14 SUNDAY · *Moon Age Day 9 · Moon Sign Leo*

You ought to be able to get a great deal done today. You have significant energy at your disposal and a general attitude to life that those around you find refreshing and interesting. This means that your influence is strong and that you can get your own way, without any sort of bullying or argument.

15 MONDAY · *Moon Age Day 10 · Moon Sign Leo*

The things you learn at work today can have an important bearing on the future as a whole. It's definitely time to keep your eyes and ears open. Even the sort of gossip that you would normally avoid is worth your attention. In a personal sense, it is the small things of life that tend to make you happy now.

16 TUESDAY · *Moon Age Day 11 · Moon Sign Virgo*

There are some dynamic influences around today and your mind is likely to be quick-fire and your reactions like lightning. Your life is going to be busy this week and there could be every opportunity to take journeys, whether these turn out to be for the sake of business of for pleasure.

17 WEDNESDAY · *Moon Age Day 12 · Moon Sign Virgo*

Lots of planetary energy is now likely to be focused on your own needs and requirements. Like all Fire signs, Aries can exhibit a slightly selfish streak from time to time, though now it appears that you help others as much as you do yourself. Confidence should not be hard to find in professional matters.

18 THURSDAY · *Moon Age Day 13 · Moon Sign Libra*

Certain setbacks are more or less inevitable today, though if you know this is going to be the case, they won't throw you too much. On the positive side, a deeper sense of reasoning should accompany this lunar low and allow you to ride out the trend. Look out for personalities entering your life.

19 FRIDAY · *Moon Age Day 14 · Moon Sign Libra*

Your progress may still be limited and at best you will make modest steps towards your objectives. Instead of putting too much effort into making material gains, you might be better off thinking about your personal life, an area that is likely to be luckier for you. Listen to the stories your loved ones are telling at present.

20 SATURDAY *Moon Age Day 15   Moon Sign Scorpio*

Your personal expectations are sometimes too high, particularly regarding your own capabilities. It might be true that you can work near-miracles occasionally but you must realistically face the fact that this is not always the case. You also don't always have the absolute support of other people. Be willing to settle for very good today, instead of amazing.

21 SUNDAY *Moon Age Day 16   Moon Sign Scorpio*

When pressing ahead with long-terms plans, you should make sure that everyone else concerned has been informed. There are people around who won't be very happy if they feel they have been bamboozled into something they don't want. It's really just a matter of sharing information and asking for opinions.

22 MONDAY *Moon Age Day 17   Moon Sign Sagittarius*

Current trends in your chart put the emphasis firmly on leisure – even though it's Monday! As a result, it's likely that for both today and the week ahead you will be looking to have fun. Such is your state of mind that it is easy for you to find ways to amuse those around you, especially your partner and friends.

23 TUESDAY *Moon Age Day 18   Moon Sign Sagittarius*

A slight shift in emphasis brings you to an outdoor frame of mind which, bearing in mind the advancing year, is probably not so much of a surprise. You will also be quite intellectually motivated and anxious to travel to places that are firmly rooted in history and which retain a heady atmosphere of the past.

24 WEDNESDAY *Moon Age Day 19   Moon Sign Capricorn*

Though you might have to overcome an initial sense of lethargy regarding career and practical matters, things soon speed up and you find yourself making significant progress. The attitude of friends could puzzle you for a while, until you manage to get them talking.

25 THURSDAY   *Moon Age Day 20   Moon Sign Capricorn*

There are plenty of good things coming your way, one or two of which you've been waiting a long time to enjoy. You should be pretty much on top of the world and anxious to make the most of whatever life is offering. This is more than can be said for someone at home or maybe a very good friend.

26 FRIDAY   *Moon Age Day 21   Moon Sign Capricorn*

Take care to avoid unnecessary conflicts with others at the end of this working week. There isn't much doubt that you will win any argument in which you take part but you will probably end up feeling bad about the situation. Better by far to stop such eventualities before they start.

27 SATURDAY   *Moon Age Day 22   Moon Sign Aquarius*

Current personal and professional developments should continue to go generally your way. If you have any difficulty at all, it could be in the sphere of your family life. Trends suggest that younger family members especially may be likely to play up, probably for no justifiable reason that you can see or understand.

28 SUNDAY   *Moon Age Day 23   Moon Sign Aquarius*

Avoid snap decisions today and be willing to go round the long way. Spending some time genuinely weighing up the pros and cons of any situation could pay real dividends and there isn't much doubt that you are able turn on the intuition when you really need to do so. Try to compromise as much as possible.

29 MONDAY   *Moon Age Day 24   Moon Sign Pisces*

It is true that you might feel a touch self-indulgent and even extravagant at present but everyone has to spoil themselves sometimes. If this worries you, turn your attention instead to romance where you are entirely giving and not counting the personal cost. Whatever you do, an interesting day lies in store.

30 TUESDAY   *Moon Age Day 25   Moon Sign Pisces*

You can almost certainly expect to be the centre of attention today. There are likely to be compliments coming in from every direction, so it may be a little hard to detect if one person is being slightly sarcastic. Aries is one of the most potent of the zodiac signs but it should always be wary of believing the hype.

2019

1 WEDNESDAY *Moon Age Day 26 Moon Sign Pisces*

It might have failed to register to such a busy person as you that the spring has more than arrived. There is a wealth of planetary trends around you at present that indicate a growing need to run barefoot through the new-grown grass. If you can't manage that, at least get a breath of good fresh air this week.

2 THURSDAY *Moon Age Day 27 Moon Sign Aries*

Your hunches are strong at the moment and you can afford to act on them. If it isn't exactly intuition you are displaying, it is calculated instinct. Analysing what makes those around you tick seems to be a piece of cake and there will be no shortage of clues to help you out. You have your wits about you during this lunar high.

3 FRIDAY *Moon Age Day 28 Moon Sign Aries*

The lunar high continues as good luck pays you a visit. Not only are your assumptions likely to be correct, but you can also look forward to making something out of them in a material sense. Time for reflection is somewhat limited because you remain extremely busy but take care not to ignore family members.

4 SATURDAY *Moon Age Day 0 Moon Sign Taurus*

There may be exciting events happening today because of the lives of loved ones. This probably means you won't be the centre of attention, and that fact might not please you at all. An abiding lesson to be learned now is that you can gain almost as much from the back of the queue as you can from the front.

5 SUNDAY
Moon Age Day 1   Moon Sign Taurus

Along comes a period during which it is quite possible for you to deal with several different tasks at the same time. Whether or not you achieve all your objectives in the way you would wish could be in doubt. What matters most is that you are happy with your lot and comfortable in your decisions.

6 MONDAY
Moon Age Day 2   Moon Sign Taurus

This is a good time to focus on creative pursuits and also to give some attention to your home surroundings. The arrival of the warmer weather might have put you in the mood to do some decorating or, if you can afford it, to supervise someone else doing it for you. Some gardening isn't entirely out of the question, even if this is not your usual hobby.

7 TUESDAY
Moon Age Day 3   Moon Sign Gemini

Among those you mix with you are the cream of the crop. Soaking up all this popularity isn't too difficult for Aries but you must not allow it to go to your head. You are such a good self-publicist that if you are not careful you might end up believing your own spin.

8 WEDNESDAY
Moon Age Day 4   Moon Sign Gemini

It isn't hard to get into the good books of others because it is so easy for you to turn on the charm. Your confidence grows when you are dealing with situations you fully understand, though is less evident when you are out on a limb. Accept that interruptions are probably inevitable today, especially as some of them should be amusing.

9 THURSDAY
Moon Age Day 5   Moon Sign Cancer

The things that others do for you at this time can make you feel very lucky indeed, even though the favours that come your way are only small in scope. Maybe you are thinking more deeply but you should find that you recognise exactly where your bread is buttered and respond positively in kind.

10 FRIDAY
Moon Age Day 6   Moon Sign Cancer

Your own personal technical skills count today, especially in the workplace. Success lies for the moment in the things you can do that others cannot. Personally speaking, you may consider yourself to be treated better at the moment than has been the case in the recent past.

11 SATURDAY
Moon Age Day 7   Moon Sign Leo

There are likely to be minor distractions around and these can definitely get in the way of your practical progress. Some of these are entirely social in nature, so eradicating them is not going to be easy without eliminating friendly contact. In the end, what you are looking for is compromise.

12 SUNDAY
Moon Age Day 8   Moon Sign Leo

Working in a team may now be less satisfying than was probably the case earlier in the month. Quite a few trends now show what an individualist you are likely to be. Stick close to people in whom you have natural confidence and don't be too quick to pass judgement on anyone's ideas for the moment.

13 MONDAY
Moon Age Day 9   Moon Sign Virgo

Look out for monetary increases. These may not be large, or come from directions you would particularly expect, but they should be useful. Some speculation could be necessary if you really want to make financial gains, but heed the warning that you are not in the best planetary position to push this too far.

14 TUESDAY
Moon Age Day 10   Moon Sign Virgo

Now is the time to exercise your intellectual powers and to show a few doubters exactly what you are capable of. Don't allow your enthusiasm to run away with you, though. There are times for taking chances and situations in which it would be foolish to gamble. Knowing the difference is what counts today.

15 WEDNESDAY *Moon Age Day 11 Moon Sign Libra*

Keep life as simple as possible today and try to realise that you will get what you need right now, though probably not quite what you want. Happiness is so often a state of mind and you are philosophical enough at present to realise this. Participating in hobbies could appeal to you now.

16 THURSDAY *Moon Age Day 12 Moon Sign Libra*

This is probably not the best time to take risks because the lunar low doesn't offer you quite the level of planetary support you might require. Be steady in your actions and think ahead. It doesn't appear that you are in any physical danger, though it is entirely possible that you could suffer a financial setback if you are not careful.

17 FRIDAY *Moon Age Day 13 Moon Sign Scorpio*

Some useful information could be coming your way, probably from directions you least expected. You are ready to take decisions in isolation if that's what it takes to get ahead. However, you are equally likely to co-operate with those who display a similar attitude.

18 SATURDAY *Moon Age Day 14 Moon Sign Scorpio*

You always enjoy a magnetic personality but never more so than appears to be the case right now. Exciting romantic developments could come along at any time and may take you by surprise. You should be happy to join in with whatever is happening in your social group and may even initiate something.

19 SUNDAY *Moon Age Day 15 Moon Sign Scorpio*

Watch out for situations that are not at all what they appear. This would not be a good day for signing documents unless you have had the time to look very carefully at them. Someone you haven't seen for ages is likely to come along at any moment now and might bring a surprise or two with them.

20 MONDAY   *Moon Age Day 16   Moon Sign Sagittarius*

Your ambitions at work could be really driving you forward now. If you are not employed or perhaps retired, you will still be finding things to keep you occupied. You seem to be embarking on some sort of personal search but it would be sensible to itemise first what you are actually looking for.

21 TUESDAY   *Moon Age Day 17   Moon Sign Sagittarius*

Work and practical matters seem capable of running themselves at the moment. Meanwhile you see ways to have a good time and to lift the spirits of someone who is not happy at present. Your confidence isn't in short supply but do make sure you know what you are talking about before you say too much.

22 WEDNESDAY   *Moon Age Day 18   Moon Sign Capricorn*

With relationships now showing a good deal more sparkle than for a while you will be happy to take more notice of them. There are all sorts of people likely to come into your life at this time, some of whom hold a particular fascination for you. Don't be too willing to fall for a glib line or an attractive face.

23 THURSDAY   *Moon Age Day 19   Moon Sign Capricorn*

Save time for creative meditation or simply for daydreaming. There will be a tendency for you to be doing some spring-cleaning around now and today is probably as good a day as any to get cracking. Even when you are really busy you will be humming a little tune or thinking about places you love.

24 FRIDAY   *Moon Age Day 20   Moon Sign Aquarius*

Friendships have much going for them now, and indeed across the weekend. You will most likely be seeing people with whom you were closer in the past and there is also the chance that you could make some new friends. Be certain to ask for something you really want – you might just get it for your cheek.

25 SATURDAY   *Moon Age Day 21   Moon Sign Aquarius*

A change of scenery for the weekend would lighten your mood no end. You won't need too much encouragement in order to have a good time and you clearly know how to encourage other people to let their hair down too. Even normally solemn types should be willing to take off their socks and paddle now.

26 SUNDAY   *Moon Age Day 22   Moon Sign Aquarius*

Strong emotions underlie what you are saying and doing today, even if some people don't understand this. It wouldn't be fair to criticise others for their treatment of you if they don't understand what they are doing wrong. To obviate the issue altogether, make sure you explain yourself fully.

27 MONDAY   *Moon Age Day 23   Moon Sign Pisces*

When it comes to getting your own way in personal relationships, you should have very little trouble at the moment. It is possible that Arians who are between relationships at the moment could see romance blossoming very soon. However, some might say you are presently too particular for your own good.

28 TUESDAY   *Moon Age Day 24   Moon Sign Pisces*

Whilst your basic ambition will tend to keep energy levels high, you are still likely to find yourself subject to an emotional and a restless mood for much of the time. It's as though you can't quite decide what you want from life, or how to go about finding the path that is going to be right for you in the future.

29 WEDNESDAY   *Moon Age Day 25   Moon Sign Aries*

Trends move on and you now enjoy an intellectual and physical peak, not to mention a time of significant popularity. With everything to play for it is almost certain you would be willing to take a few chances, though this probably isn't necessary in order to get more or less what you want from life.

30 THURSDAY
Moon Age Day 26   Moon Sign Aries

Help comes from some very unexpected places right now and it appears that some major ambitions are likely to be achieved either now or in the very near future. Getting your mind around problems that have taxed you in the past now seems a piece of cake. However, take care not to ignore too many rules and regulations.

31 FRIDAY
Moon Age Day 27   Moon Sign Aries

Your personal charisma is now very strong and it is unlikely that many could resist it. This may lead to you stealing the spotlight from others, something you occasionally do unintentionally. Yours can be a very dominant character but you are sensitive too, so make sure you don't deliberately upstage anyone.

June

2019

1 SATURDAY
Moon Age Day 28   Moon Sign Taurus

Opt for some light relief if at all possible because this is not a day on which you ought to take yourself or anyone else too seriously. In a social sense you can lighten the load of a number of different individuals, as well as taking the sting out of a situation that could otherwise lead to unnecessary arguments.

2 SUNDAY
Moon Age Day 29   Moon Sign Taurus

There could be scope for some shortcuts to better prospects, particularly in terms of family finances. This is not the only matter on your mind however, because much of today is about having a good time. The most important fact to remember at present is not to take yourself or anyone else too seriously.

3 MONDAY
Moon Age Day 0   Moon Sign Gemini

Some distractions are likely today, particularly when it comes to your professional life. Perhaps funnier than the weekend, this Monday almost certainly promises entertainment, much of which is inspired by your own efforts. New friends are there for the taking.

4 TUESDAY
Moon Age Day 1   Moon Sign Gemini

It could seem that the pressure is on in personal or domestic situations, which means talking more to family members and probably making a few concessions on the way. Situations in a practical and professional sense move on relentlessly, but you are very much more in command than you might think.

5 WEDNESDAY
Moon Age Day 2   Moon Sign Cancer

This is another beneficial time for showing a progressive face to potential changes. These can come upon you in a number of different ways and you see them on the horizon. It would be better to take command now rather than to leave any situation until it becomes the driving force that overtakes you.

6 THURSDAY
Moon Age Day 3   Moon Sign Cancer

There is potential for at least some muddled thinking today, which is why it would be sensible to check over a few facts and figures with others before you commit yourself to any widespread alterations to your life. In any case, tomorrow would be far better for making important decisions of almost any sort.

7 FRIDAY
Moon Age Day 4   Moon Sign Leo

It is clear that your imagination is working overtime at the moment and that you have little ability to change that situation. This might lead you to contemplate some rather unlikely and possibly even potentially troubling scenarios, but it may also offer you an insight into the future that is more than useful.

8 SATURDAY
Moon Age Day 5   Moon Sign Leo

There is no need at all to assume that things are going wrong simply because life might be rather quiet at the beginning of the weekend. It is really up to you to add both the events and the incentives today. This would be an excellent time for a shopping spree, as trends seem to indicate some bargains in the offing.

9 SUNDAY
Moon Age Day 6   Moon Sign Virgo

People around you, especially at home, should be doing all they can to make you happy at present, which means that much of your attention can be focused elsewhere. Don't be too quick to cast judgement over anything and be willing to offer sound advice, but only when you are asked for it.

10 MONDAY   *Moon Age Day 7   Moon Sign Virgo*

Some of your more grandiose expectations will have to be played down today, otherwise there could be some ensuing disappointments on the way. Simply remain realistic in your approach to life and don't be too willing to take a point of view that others would see as being both radical and probably unworkable.

11 TUESDAY   *Moon Age Day 8   Moon Sign Virgo*

It's good to be out there amongst peer groups, steering the course of the future, not only for yourself but for them too. People expect you to take a leading role in a number of different existing projects and others you are thinking up for yourself. Aries is particularly innovative at this time so don't hold back.

12 WEDNESDAY   *Moon Age Day 9   Moon Sign Libra*

Today is best served by taking life steadily. There is nothing to be gained at present from pushing yourself too hard and a contemplative approach to most situations will work out best. Finances would respond to a special overview on your part, but not to any drastic action at the present time.

13 THURSDAY   *Moon Age Day 10   Moon Sign Libra*

Many Arians are deliberately taking a holiday from responsibility right now. There are plenty of people around you who have social invitations, though it is almost certain that you would want to spend at least some time on your own. It isn't that you are depressed, merely quieter than usual.

14 FRIDAY   *Moon Age Day 11   Moon Sign Scorpio*

There are still some tensions about that you could successfully address if you put your mind to it today. If you find yourself needing to go along with a specific point of view, do so without any doubt in your mind. Most people, especially family members, will be happy to opt for a good time, which it is within your power to offer.

15 SATURDAY   *Moon Age Day 12   Moon Sign Scorpio*

If you have any problems today, take them to people you know. Once again you fare best when spending time with those you trust. The outside world can seem somehow unnerving at present, even though this is nothing but a temporary phase. Be willing to share a new idea with someone who is genuinely interested.

16 SUNDAY   *Moon Age Day 13   Moon Sign Sagittarius*

Trends suggest that there could be some slight confusion regarding the actions of others, especially family members. It's really important now to talk things through and to make certain in your own mind that you know how nearest and dearest are likely to react under any given circumstances.

17 MONDAY   *Moon Age Day 14   Moon Sign Sagittarius*

Today's sources of joy and pleasure should be with regard to friends and colleagues, most of whom are doing what they can to be supportive of your ideas and plans. This isn't exclusively the case but there is no reason whatsoever today to defend yourself before you are attacked in any way.

18 TUESDAY   *Moon Age Day 15   Moon Sign Capricorn*

Discussions with others prove to be quite pleasing now and can lead you in the direction of some interesting new ideas. Avoid petty little conflicts, particularly with people who are going to be necessary to your success in a very short period of time. Stand by a decision you made recently.

19 WEDNESDAY   *Moon Age Day 16   Moon Sign Capricorn*

You may now have an overwhelming desire to meet new and interesting people and to take your life down completely fresh avenues. There isn't anything especially unusual or remarkable about this. You can put some of it down to the time of year and the rest to your Arian personality.

20 THURSDAY   *Moon Age Day 17   Moon Sign Capricorn*

At home or even out and about amongst friends, there is still the slight danger that what you are saying and what you mean are two different things. It is crucial that you explain yourself properly and that everyone understands the way you feel. Look out for an improvement in your finances.

21 FRIDAY   *Moon Age Day 18   Moon Sign Aquarius*

If you can work in a group this should go in your favour, as this is a time when co-operation comes as second nature to you. If you are involved in any sort of business partnership, you should now find that the common ideas being thrown up prove to be the most useful. The attitude of an acquaintance could be puzzling later in the day.

22 SATURDAY   *Moon Age Day 19   Moon Sign Aquarius*

It is extremely important that you analyse and understand your own thought processes if you want to succeed in anything, both now and in the days ahead. Instead of taking anything for granted, check and double-check your facts. Don't sign any contract today unless you have read it very carefully.

23 SUNDAY   *Moon Age Day 20   Moon Sign Pisces*

Someone really needs your assistance today and Sunday should offer you plenty of time to attend to them. Aries is often extremely busy and saying those things that are most important, especially in a romantic attachment, is sometimes forgotten. Curb your sense of adventure and settle for a family and personal day.

24 MONDAY   *Moon Age Day 21   Moon Sign Pisces*

Don't press the action button of your life too much at this time. Instead take time to allow situations to wash over you much more than you usually would, even if to do so seems somehow tedious. There is plenty of time to get on with what you want later. For now, take a little break.

25 TUESDAY *Moon Age Day 22 Moon Sign Pisces*

This is now a day to buckle down and to get on with routines. You may not care very much for these but they will prove to be very important in practical matters. Don't be too quick to jump to conclusions in a professional sense, but instead bide your time and wait for situations to mature before passing judgement.

26 WEDNESDAY *Moon Age Day 23 Moon Sign Aries*

Feelings of intense generosity may come not only from the lunar high but also on account of some strong planetary interplay. You want to do whatever you can to help others and can prove to be a dominant moving force behind charitable and philanthropic gestures of many kinds.

27 THURSDAY *Moon Age Day 24 Moon Sign Aries*

You can talk almost anyone into anything at this time, though you will almost certainly restrict yourself to individuals who seem to have been taking a somewhat shaky path of late. In addition, you are funny and very resourceful. Altogether, this is a winning combination for this stage of the working week.

28 FRIDAY *Moon Age Day 25 Moon Sign Taurus*

This is a day during when it is very important to avoid any sort of misunderstanding. It is possible that you fail to get your message across when it is most important, which can lead to all manner of complications later. This isn't usually the way of Aries but you need to double-check your own assumptions right now.

29 SATURDAY *Moon Age Day 26 Moon Sign Taurus*

You may expect a progressive day at work, though this won't help you much unless you work at the weekend. Domestically speaking, you really won't be in the mood and will want to leave home-based matters in the hands of others. Avoid a feeling of dissatisfaction by keeping physically active.

30 SUNDAY

Moon Age Day 27   Moon Sign Gemini

You are likely to be extremely busy today and may fail to find the necessary time to let those important people in your life know how special their presence actually is to you. Think about this and make sure that you spend just a few minutes now and again letting them know. It really is important at this stage of the month.

♈ July

2019

1 MONDAY
Moon Age Day 28   Moon Sign Gemini

If you are not carefully organised today, there really is a chance that an extremely good plan could fail to get off the drawing board. Look well ahead of yourself and plan carefully. If you feel it is necessary to enlist the support of someone in the know don't be shy of doing so.

2 TUESDAY
Moon Age Day 0   Moon Sign Gemini

You are impatient to see your ideas becoming realities but you can't rush any situation today. Take things slowly and steadily, making sure that you have dealt with every contingency. Creating the necessary mental space to dream some important dreams is another factor you can't dismiss today.

3 WEDNESDAY
Moon Age Day 1   Moon Sign Cancer

This is a very light-hearted period, during which you are pleased to meet new people. You are jovial and approachable at present and should enjoy a degree of popularity. People from the dim and distant past could be making a return visit to your life before very long.

4 THURSDAY
Moon Age Day 2   Moon Sign Cancer

Rewards come via the broadening of your general horizons and through travel. This would be an excellent time for Arians to take a holiday, or merely to get away from the everyday for a few hours. Almost any sort of journey would suit you, as long as it is undertaken for fun.

5 FRIDAY
Moon Age Day 3   Moon Sign Leo

This is a period with plenty of opportunities for intimate get-togethers. If you had already decided that the time was right for a heart-to-heart talk with someone, now is the day for it. Your level of tolerance is much higher than it sometimes is and you positively revel in situations that demand a great deal of you.

6 SATURDAY
Moon Age Day 4   Moon Sign Leo

If you have a bee in your bonnet regarding a specific matter, you should do something about it before the weekend grows very old. With an overdose of confidence, you are likely to take on all sorts of jobs that you would normally leave to experts. That's fine, but do check out the details before you get cracking.

7 SUNDAY
Moon Age Day 5   Moon Sign Virgo

Current influences place great emphasis on the social side of your life. You could enjoy travelling far and wide at the moment, but it really depends if you can find the time to do so. The fact is that you are likely to be very busy in a host of different ways and there certainly won't be any opportunity to get bored.

8 MONDAY
☿   *Moon Age Day 6   Moon Sign Virgo*

Life is likely to be stimulating and particularly eventful at the moment. There is just a slight tendency for you to feel that you are going round in circles regarding specific issues but the truth is that you are more capable than believe yourself to be. Catching up with a few chores could prove to be more interesting than you expect.

9 TUESDAY
☿   *Moon Age Day 7   Moon Sign Libra*

There could be a few disruptions around today, either emotional or material. For this you can thank the lunar low and you can only really avoid such eventualities by spending a considerable part of the day on your own. This does not suit Aries at all, so prepare to face a slight dilemma.

10 WEDNESDAY ☿   *Moon Age Day 8   Moon Sign Libra*

Various tests of your patience are apt to show up today. Since the typical Arian is not famed for his or her tolerance, you can expect to have to work that much harder at the moment. There are possible gains coming from friendship, plus the hint of better times for some of you when it comes to love.

11 THURSDAY   ☿   *Moon Age Day 9   Moon Sign Scorpio*

Teamwork situations are quite useful and look likely to be immensely enjoyable across the weekend to come. Today, you might feel slightly lacking in energy, particularly later in the day, but that won't prevent you from scoring a number of successes. In social situations, move over to allow someone else to take the limelight.

12 FRIDAY   ☿   *Moon Age Day 10   Moon Sign Scorpio*

Get as practical as you like today because it is that side of your nature that is working so well. Although you could find relatives difficult to deal with, in the main you remain certain of potential gains and anxious to please. What shows most of all today is a friendly and warm nature.

13 SATURDAY   ☿ *Moon Age Day 11   Moon Sign Sagittarius*

The pursuit of outdoor interests should make the day go with a swing, particularly if you don't have to work. Although you are now quite competitive, this doesn't really extend to professional matters. With no real sense of ultimate responsibility at present, you really only want to have some fun.

14 SUNDAY   ☿ *Moon Age Day 12   Moon Sign Sagittarius*

Your ability to get the best from life in a social sense is enviable. Popularity is now your middle name and you find yourself centre stage in a number of different ways. If it seems as though someone is only just beginning to realise your true potential, this could be because your own headlights are turned up so bright now.

15 MONDAY ☿ *Moon Age Day 13*   *Moon Sign Capricorn*

Life is now altogether more interesting across the board, and is made better still by the presence of people who are really important to you. There are moments today when you might doubt your own capabilities though in the end you should come up trumps. The planets have a tip for today: listen to the advice of friends.

16 TUESDAY ☿ *Moon Age Day 14*   *Moon Sign Capricorn*

Emotional relationships still provide the most comfortable associations, while your professional life appears to be on hold just for the moment. The present planetary line-up shows that you might be about to spill the beans over an issue you have kept quiet about for ages – if this rings true to you, be careful who you tell.

17 WEDNESDAY ☿ *Moon Age Day 15*   *Moon Sign Capricorn*

Encounters with those you feel to be on the same wavelength as you should prove very rewarding indeed and could bring you to a better understanding of situations that have confused you in the past. Don't stick around in the same place today and do what you can to travel around a little.

18 THURSDAY ☿ *Moon Age Day 16*   *Moon Sign Aquarius*

There seem to be forces at work that are helping you get more of what you want in a financial sense, though this isn't something you should push at the moment as trends also firmly suggest that you should take care with spending. Planning for the shorter term is probably better than trying to look too far ahead for now at least.

19 FRIDAY ☿ *Moon Age Day 17*   *Moon Sign Aquarius*

Personal freedom is what seems to matter the most now, which is not at all unusual for Aries. You need to do your own thing, which might go against the grain as far as certain other people are concerned. That cannot be avoided because you will soon tire and start to fail if you feel fettered.

20 SATURDAY ☿ *Moon Age Day 18   Moon Sign Pisces*

Some hopeful news might be coming from far off places and this could involve information regarding journeys you are likely to be making yourself before long. Keep an eye on your romantic partner and make certain that he or she understands how deep your caring goes. There might be some confusion about this right now.

21 SUNDAY ☿ *Moon Age Day 19   Moon Sign Pisces*

Avoid those who sound too good to be true today because there is a real chance that your intuition is quite correct. Deceptive types might be few and far between, but there could still be a few glib lines around. Those with the zodiac sign of Aries should easily be able to recognise them and avoid the problems that can result.

22 MONDAY ☿ *Moon Age Day 20   Moon Sign Pisces*

Don't sit on the fence today. You may need to take a stance, even if this means making yourself slightly unpopular with someone. It won't be possible to agree with everyone and you will be much better off once you have committed yourself one way or another. Trust your own judgement in matters, both business and personal.

23 TUESDAY ☿ *Moon Age Day 21   Moon Sign Aries*

This should be a time of great energy and not a little good luck. If you have been planning events for today, you can be sure they will go ahead with a definite swing. Don't give up on efforts that might recently have seemed hopeless. You can move mountains now, or at least pretty large hills.

24 WEDNESDAY ☿ *Moon Age Day 22   Moon Sign Aries*

The good times are likely to continue for most Arians, marred only slightly for some by a tendency to be a little too big for your own boots. If you avoid this, the world is likely to be your oyster and there isn't much to hold you back. Relatives and friends alike are supportive and loving but not as much as your partner.

25 THURSDAY ☿ *Moon Age Day 23* *Moon Sign Taurus*

A fulfilling period in terms of romance and pleasure seems to be the case as Thursday stands in view. Anything old, unusual or curious is likely to captivate you now and you also have a great fondness for intellectual pursuits. There may be strong support for your ideas coming from unexpected places.

26 FRIDAY ☿ *Moon Age Day 24* *Moon Sign Taurus*

Remember that there is only so much you can control on a practical level and you might need to rely on the advice and skills of someone who is more in the know than you are. Admitting you may be out of your depth isn't easy but could be necessary if you want to really get ahead in the next couple of days.

27 SATURDAY ☿ *Moon Age Day 25* *Moon Sign Taurus*

Make time for simpler pleasures this weekend. If you try to push too hard in a practical sense you will no doubt come unstuck. The best of all worlds would be to spend more time today with family members and especially your partner. You can expect to feel the need to be surrounded by those you trust.

28 SUNDAY ☿ *Moon Age Day 26* *Moon Sign Gemini*

Try to make this a very special day for yourself and your nearest and dearest. Although practical matters have a lot going for them, it is in the sphere of personal attachments and family values that you continue to find the greatest happiness. This is a Sunday that was built for enjoyment and for showing your true feelings.

29 MONDAY ☿ *Moon Age Day 27* *Moon Sign Gemini*

The emphasis is now on work, but that doesn't mean you are forgetting to focus on your home life on occasions too. Spend some time helping a loved one, even if they haven't exactly asked for your support. This is also a time during which you will want to learn something new, so search out some details.

30 TUESDAY ☿ *Moon Age Day 28 Moon Sign Cancer*

You are likely to be right in the middle of the social mainstream around now; happy to shine and eager to let others know you are around. Not everyone rates you but it's impossible to be an Aries and to get through life without one or two people showing a little jealousy or envy towards you.

31 WEDNESDAY ☿ *Moon Age Day 0 Moon Sign Cancer*

Today you would be better off as part of a group because you will draw strength from others and get on much better than if you were working alone. There are some definite gains to be made that involve you putting forward some fairly radical proposals and then watching for the reactions. The most important element for you now is flexibility.

August 2019

1 THURSDAY
Moon Age Day 1   Moon Sign Leo

The pleasure principle is writ large today and you take a break from the mundane as you seek ways to please yourself. A little luxury is fine, just as long as you don't take things too far. Some interesting people cross your path at the moment. One or two of them may even be famous in some way.

2 FRIDAY
Moon Age Day 2   Moon Sign Leo

The planetary focus now is on your strong personality. People should be quite happy to defer to you in most situations, just as long as you maintain that air of total self-confidence. Generally speaking, this should be easy, though there may be one or two moments today during which you are not entirely sure of yourself.

3 SATURDAY
Moon Age Day 3   Moon Sign Virgo

You may be struggling to come to terms with a personal issue. If this turns out to be the case, talk things through carefully and don't allow your ego to get in the way. It isn't always easy for you to eat humble pie, but a small portion would not go amiss now. The whole world will love you for it.

4 SUNDAY
Moon Age Day 4   Moon Sign Virgo

Although this day is less satisfying in terms of overall success, you can get what you want in less obvious ways. Some people might call your present behaviour a little sneaky, but that is probably because they didn't think up your strategy first. It is possible to score successes, but by using psychology, not force.

5 MONDAY
Moon Age Day 5   Moon Sign Libra

Assistance for practical projects can come from a number of different directions, all of which you need to heed if you want to get the most from life. This Monday can bring a few temporary frustrations, particularly at work, but these should not be overplayed in your mind. It is important to keep your eye on the ball.

6 TUESDAY
Moon Age Day 6   Moon Sign Libra

A degree of assistance never goes amiss, and this is what you can expect if you are an Arian who is working today. The same is generally true in non-professional situations, though in this case you are in a better position to help yourself. Get unsavoury jobs out of the way as early in the day as you can.

7 WEDNESDAY
Moon Age Day 7   Moon Sign Scorpio

You will have to keep a closer eye on your budget now because you are inclined to squander money at the very time you need it the most. An investment in travel could pay handsome dividends, if only in terms of your pleasure. With the weekend not too far off, you may decide the time is right to change location.

8 THURSDAY
Moon Age Day 8   Moon Sign Scorpio

There might be a downside to matters associated with love. Affairs of the heart are not the best-supported aspect of life today, thanks to the present planetary line up. Perhaps you don't fully understand what your partner is trying to say to you, or else their attitude is one that proves a mystery at the moment.

9 FRIDAY
Moon Age Day 9   Moon Sign Sagittarius

There are many comings and goings, leading to some confusion and uncertainty in specific areas of your life. This is likely to go against the grain and you will probably do everything you can to bring more discipline into your life. In discussions, avoid arguing any sort of negative case and focus on the positive.

10 SATURDAY   *Moon Age Day 10   Moon Sign Sagittarius*

It is towards the domestic side of life that your mind is apt to turn at the present time. The weekend finds you paying specific attention to details in and around your home, but the fact that August often allows greater movement might also mean your mind is geared towards thoughts of holidays.

11 SUNDAY   *Moon Age Day 11   Moon Sign Sagittarius*

In personal relationships, you have your work cut out today. It is possible that your partner is behaving in a less than typical manner, whilst you do not show quite the level of patience that would normally be the case. Make a special effort to show that you care, and that your heart is in the right place.

12 MONDAY   *Moon Age Day 12   Moon Sign Capricorn*

Financial consolidation and security are highlighted at the beginning of a new working week. Right now, you are a better saver than spender, because thoughts of long-term security are on your mind. Maybe you are adopting a slightly modified mind set, which not everyone is going to understand.

13 TUESDAY   *Moon Age Day 13   Moon Sign Capricorn*

This ought to be a stable and productive time, particularly in terms of your personal life. It is now much easier to show the people you love that you are sincere and working towards their best interests. Insincerity is not part of your agenda, and now it is possible to prove this fact.

14 WEDNESDAY   *Moon Age Day 14   Moon Sign Aquarius*

A problem-solving day would probably be fun, and it ought to be quite successful under present trends. You now have the ability to go to the heart of any matter and to deal with details in a flash. On a more personal footing, you will want to prove just how deep and enduring your love actually is.

15 THURSDAY *Moon Age Day 15   Moon Sign Aquarius*

This is a day when it ought to be easy to make money. You are ingenious at present and have a number of different schemes in mind. From a social point of view you welcome the company of interesting and stimulating people, as well as mixing freely with those you haven't met before.

16 FRIDAY *Moon Age Day 16   Moon Sign Aquarius*

Variety is certainly the spice of life today. You won't take kindly to being held back in any way and it appears you are pushing yourself just as hard as is necessary in your efforts to get ahead. What shines out most of all is your power of communication, which is second to none at this stage of the year.

17 SATURDAY *Moon Age Day 17   Moon Sign Pisces*

This is a good time for making financial gains and for getting your own way in both professional and personal matters. When you are asked to do something you haven't attempted before, don't automatically expect that there will be complications. You are more versatile than you think.

18 SUNDAY *Moon Age Day 18   Moon Sign Pisces*

You wish to express your self-confidence in new ways and there are few astrological restrictions around on this Sunday. Getting on well with just about anyone should prove to be a piece of cake and you find yourself in a position to bask in the glory that comes from doing things right first time, every time.

19 MONDAY *Moon Age Day 19   Moon Sign Aries*

Life tends to be highly fulfilling now and with a better than average amount of good luck around, you can make the best of most situations. You might find it hard to resist the temptation to move away from normal routines, but the vast majority of tasks can easily wait until later.

20 TUESDAY
Moon Age Day 20   Moon Sign Aries

Changes are now inevitable, and you will want to revitalise aspects of your professional life that have not been working all that well recently. You might be surprised by the way certain people are treating you, probably because they are developing a new respect for your acumen.

21 WEDNESDAY
Moon Age Day 21   Moon Sign Aries

This is a good time for keeping your eyes and ears open. With new incentives coming from a host of different directions and with plenty to keep you busy, today should pass by in a flash. Keep in mind, though, that not everyone has your best interests at heart and there could be at least one person who doesn't mean you well.

22 THURSDAY
Moon Age Day 22   Moon Sign Taurus

Communication increases at the same speed as curiosity and both are well marked in your day. With plenty of people to call upon and a great desire to push the bounds of the possible, you are making a good impression. Your popularity is off the scale and the chances of progress increase considerably.

23 FRIDAY
Moon Age Day 23   Moon Sign Taurus

Your ability to express yourself is never lacking but at the moment it proves to be more powerful than ever. Active and enthusiastic, you are also likely to be more sporting and to show a strong competitive edge. Don't forget the needs of a friend who is seeking your advice.

24 SATURDAY
Moon Age Day 24   Moon Sign Gemini

Professionally speaking, it seems likely that you will want to make a new plan of action. Although there may be little you can actually do about this if you don't work on a Saturday, you can at least get your thinking head on. Don't be too quick to judge the actions or opinions of others today because you could later find yourself in the same boat.

25 SUNDAY *Moon Age Day 25   Moon Sign Gemini*

You have extra energy now, which you can use to work hard and to continue to make the sort of impression that proves to be so important at the moment. Avoid unnecessary rows, especially with family members or friends. Even if others bring issues to the surface, you don't have to react to them.

26 MONDAY *Moon Age Day 26   Moon Sign Cancer*

Although you are running fast at the moment it is still worth taking some time to think things through. Considering the implications of your intended actions may lead you to make slight modifications and these could prove very important in the longer-term. The attitude of your partner may be puzzling but quite delightful.

27 TUESDAY *Moon Age Day 27   Moon Sign Cancer*

When careful leadership skills are required, you will be around to show your mettle. Most people like you at present and the odd one who doesn't is out on a limb, so in a way they don't really count. There isn't much chance of you running out of steam today and life seems geared to help you out.

28 WEDNESDAY *Moon Age Day 28   Moon Sign Leo*

You ought to have the ability to communicate effectively today, even if you are dealing with subject matter you don't understand too well. Acting on impulse is slightly less advisable than has been the case for quite some time but you can still bring a great deal of enjoyment into your life and that of others.

29 THURSDAY *Moon Age Day 29   Moon Sign Leo*

Information received today could prove to be very significant, so it is extremely important to keep your eyes and ears fully open. This looks like an interesting time, with travel a possibility and the accent on excitement for young or young-at-heart Arians. Impulsive actions are once again more likely now.

30 FRIDAY
Moon Age Day 0   Moon Sign Virgo

Moneymaking ventures are at the forefront of your mind again now but they won't be the most important factor today. It is more or less certain that personal attachments and your view of them are taking centre stage in your life as a whole. As always at this time of year the call of another horizon is strong.

31 SATURDAY
Moon Age Day 1   Moon Sign Virgo

What you hear from others at this time proves vital to your progress in the medium and long-term. Although you might not have quite the ability to move around that you would wish, you can make a good deal of enjoyment wherever you happen to be. Things tend to fall into place almost automatically.

September 2019

1 SUNDAY
Moon Age Day 2   Moon Sign Libra

There can be emotional issues that need dealing with around now, a fact that might lead to some lack of progress at a time when things are generally working out fine for you. Don't worry because any complications will be short-lived. If you work on a Sunday your professionalism could reach legendary levels!

2 MONDAY
Moon Age Day 3   Moon Sign Libra

The lunar low moves away by mid afternoon, leaving you feeling slightly more positive about life in general and certainly willing to make the most of relationships. The closer you are to any given individual, the greater is the joy you presently take from their company. You have the power to turn a few new heads too.

3 TUESDAY
Moon Age Day 4   Moon Sign Scorpio

At work especially, you find plenty to do today, though if you are between jobs, or perhaps retired, you will still keep yourself very busy. Not everyone appears to have your best interests at heart at the moment but it is easy for you to spot people who are trying to complicate your life and therefore to avoid them.

4 WEDNESDAY
Moon Age Day 5   Moon Sign Scorpio

Prepare for some unaccountable setbacks today and you should find that you are able to take these in your stride. Life is fairly competitive, something from which Aries will not shy away, but the pressure this brings can tire you more quickly than normal. What you need for the end of the day is some sort of alternative activity to relax your mind.

5 THURSDAY
Moon Age Day 6   Moon Sign Scorpio

You should be happy to accept any social invitations and at the same time, you know how to make those around you happy. In a practical sense, any job you don't particularly relish at the moment ought to be got out of the way early in the day, leaving the decks clear for more pleasurable action.

6 FRIDAY
Moon Age Day 7   Moon Sign Sagittarius

Although there might be a few ups and downs at home right now, you should be able to take these in your stride. If things really get out of hand, the worst-case scenario is that you will actively choose to spend social hours with friends, rather than relatives. People in the wider world should be very giving towards you at present.

7 SATURDAY
Moon Age Day 8   Moon Sign Sagittarius

On a practical level, you cannot afford to take anything for granted today. Check and recheck facts, especially where travel plans are concerned. If you feel restless at the moment, it is important to alter things a little. Maybe a total change of scene would do you good, preferably in the company of your partner.

8 SUNDAY
Moon Age Day 9   Moon Sign Capricorn

There are situations in life today that you cannot take for granted, or problems will dog your footsteps. Take the time to look carefully at your actions and to think deeply ahead of any move. Avoid rash decisions and, if possible, qualify your own thoughts by running them past people you consider to be wise.

9 MONDAY
Moon Age Day 10   Moon Sign Capricorn

As long as you are well organised today, particularly at work, you should find life going pretty much your way. Your results may not be startling, but then you don't really worry too much about making giant leaps right now. Personal attachments should be comfortable and new relationships are maturing.

10 TUESDAY   *Moon Age Day 11   Moon Sign Aquarius*

Avoid being side-tracked by trivia if at all possible today. There is so much red tape around you should carry a pair of scissors with you, at least in a mental sense! Focus on your ability to see through to the heart of situations and then to act accordingly. Don't be put off by people who seek to confuse you.

11 WEDNESDAY   *Moon Age Day 12   Moon Sign Aquarius*

Forget modest achievements today and go for gold. This might mean taking a chance or two, but the prospect will not daunt you in the slightest. Routines are for the birds at the moment and you choose to do almost everything in your own, inimitable way. Aries is fun to be around at present, so make use of this fact.

12 THURSDAY   *Moon Age Day 13   Moon Sign Aquarius*

Other people seem to become more assertive in relation to your own desire to get ahead. If you don't heed this warning, this could mean locking horns with a couple of opponents, which actually is not necessary at all. You have more than enough mental skill at the moment to defeat anyone, simply by using some subtle psychology.

13 FRIDAY   *Moon Age Day 14   Moon Sign Pisces*

There are some potential high spots in romance this Friday, which many Arians will not want to miss. Although you are busy planning strategies, make sure to take some time out to have fun, or else all the effort is a waste of time. Getting ahead professionally is a means to an end, and not an end in itself today.

14 SATURDAY   *Moon Age Day 15   Moon Sign Pisces*

New initiatives are on the way in the romantic department of your life. Perhaps you are now looking at an existing relationship in a different light or in some cases finding a new love. Family pressures look likely to be somewhat reduced now and you make most decisions intuitively today.

15 SUNDAY   *Moon Age Day 16   Moon Sign Aries*

You can think big today and tend to make the world your oyster through the sheer dynamism of your personality. Almost anyone you meet can be both good to know and useful to have around in a practical sense. What really sets the day apart is the fact that you should be smiling nearly all the time.

16 MONDAY   *Moon Age Day 17   Moon Sign Aries*

Lady Luck seems to offer you a hand just when you need it although in reality much of the good fortune that comes your way today is created by you. What really matters the most is that last little bit of effort that gets you past the winning post. You should find most people easy to get along with at present.

17 TUESDAY   *Moon Age Day 18   Moon Sign Aries*

You may be determined to acquire money and to buy more and more things this week because the material qualities of your sign are especially highlighted. However, you won't have to look very far to see that to adopt this strategy totally would be both counterproductive and short sighted. Instead, look out for new love today.

18 WEDNESDAY   *Moon Age Day 19   Moon Sign Taurus*

You might have ideas about getting ahead that prove to be less than workable under present circumstances. Don't worry because there are people around you who have some good ideas. Taken together with your own know-how a possible collaboration could prove to be extremely lucrative in the fullness of time.

19 THURSDAY   *Moon Age Day 20   Moon Sign Taurus*

Improved resourcefulness and material values can lead to a better sense of financial security. This would be a very good time to go shopping and to hunt out a few bargains. Being in the company of exciting people is part of what today proves to be about so seek out your most adventurous friends.

20 FRIDAY   *Moon Age Day 21   Moon Sign Gemini*

Money-wise this could prove to be a more fortunate period than you might have expected. Greater success comes through prudent investment and since you might be searching for a few quieter days, this might be a good time to get your head round such matters. Don't be too quick to jump to conclusions in romance.

21 SATURDAY   *Moon Age Day 22   Moon Sign Gemini*

There is plenty of scope now for doing things the way you want and an almost immediate change in the way your mind is working. The true Aries is in evidence and your optimism is well marked. The attitude and actions of strangers might surprise you as the day wears on.

22 SUNDAY   *Moon Age Day 23   Moon Sign Gemini*

The focus is now on your family life, a fact that might not surprise you on a Sunday at this time of the year. The nights are drawing in and thoughts of the way you can improve things at home to suit you better are bound to be flooding in at any time now. You are still active and enterprising, though maybe slightly less so.

23 MONDAY   *Moon Age Day 24   Moon Sign Cancer*

Along comes a period during which your desire for material success is extremely well marked. Don't be too quick to take chances though, because in terms of money the planets suggest that you need to take a longer-term view and be willing to listen to the timely advice of professional colleagues. Love could come knocking for some Arians later in the day.

24 TUESDAY   *Moon Age Day 25   Moon Sign Cancer*

This is an excellent time for social gatherings and for getting your head round events that are coming to a head. Make sure that you make time for love in your life, especially so if you have only recently embarked on a new relationship. Don't be too quick to jump to conclusions where money is concerned.

25 WEDNESDAY
Moon Age Day 26   Moon Sign Leo

A socially helpful period allows you to enjoy your present popularity, whilst at the same time turning casual conversations into concrete ways of getting ahead in life. Don't allow discussions to turn into arguments, even if you have little or nothing to do with the way they commence.

26 THURSDAY
Moon Age Day 27   Moon Sign Leo

Listen to what those around you are saying, particularly your life partner. He or she is likely to have some very good ideas at present. These, taken together with your own ability to make reality from fantasy prove to be extremely important. Trends also suggest that someone you haven't seen for ages could be visiting your life again.

27 FRIDAY
Moon Age Day 28   Moon Sign Virgo

This is an excellent period for socialising and for bringing your plans to fruition. Mixing business with pleasure could be quite easy and you may get the opportunity to start down a new path towards an alternative form of success. Romance is possible but you simply can't push this issue at present.

28 SATURDAY
Moon Age Day 0   Moon Sign Virgo

Saturday brings a desire to spend time with family members and to do something you see as being essentially interesting. You shouldn't be too quick to jump to conclusions and a degree of circumspection would also be sensible. There are advantages to looking at specific situations in isolation around now.

29 SUNDAY
Moon Age Day 1   Moon Sign Libra

You can expect your confidence to sag a little while the lunar low is around, and there probably isn't all that much you can do to counter the situation. Simply jog along pleasantly but don't feel that you have to move any mountains. It is better by far today to pick one job and to do it properly.

30 MONDAY

Moon Age Day 2   Moon Sign Libra

You won't get everything you want this Monday, but a great deal depends on your initial expectations. If you are modest in your assessment of possibilities, you can still take pleasure in the day. Stay away from major decisions and opt instead for a strongly social day, with lots of interaction.

October 2019

1 TUESDAY
Moon Age Day 3   Moon Sign Scorpio

Today you could seek out inspiration from new contacts, as well as getting a great deal from people who figure in your life more prominently. Personal relationships should also be looking good and you have more than a slight chance of getting ahead of the game in the financial stakes. A good day all round.

2 WEDNESDAY
Moon Age Day 4   Moon Sign Scorpio

It should be easy to get where you want to be as you are in a particularly good position to pick up on the support of colleagues, a few of whom may think you are the bee's knees at present. A few unforced errors are possible but such is your nature that you manage to get yourself out of them without a struggle.

3 THURSDAY
Moon Age Day 5   Moon Sign Sagittarius

Social matters and tasks undertaken as part of a team are favourably highlighted now, leading to a feeling that you can get on well with the world at large. Perhaps you are particularly considerate regarding the feelings of those around you? Aries is also getting quite creative at this time so a spur-of-the-moment decorating spree at home is not out of the question!

4 FRIDAY
Moon Age Day 6   Moon Sign Sagittarius

Although this won't be the most eventful day of the month, it does offer potential when it comes to thinking things through. With an absence of specific events and not too much excitement to deal with, you have an uncluttered perspective. That's got to be a first, so use it wisely.

5 SATURDAY   *Moon Age Day 7   Moon Sign Capricorn*

The friendly assistance that comes from the direction of people you know, as well as strangers, is bound to be especially well received today. This ought to be a bright and breezy sort of day, without too much in the way of perceived responsibility but with plenty of entertainment and fun to brighten up your weekend.

6 SUNDAY   *Moon Age Day 8   Moon Sign Capricorn*

You might be kept in the dark regarding the plan of action that others are laying down. It really is up to you to make sure that you are not ignored and that your point of view gets an airing. If this means being even nosier than usual, then so be it. There is also a chance that some strong new personalities could enter your life around now.

7 MONDAY   *Moon Age Day 9   Moon Sign Capricorn*

It is possible that you are thinking of number one at the beginning of this working week. Your sign is sometimes accused of being selfish, though the truth is that you are merely single-minded. It wouldn't do any harm today to remember that there are other people involved in your decisions.

8 TUESDAY   *Moon Age Day 10   Moon Sign Aquarius*

While concentration on detailed work could suffer today, generally you are up for fun. It won't be easy to do everything you would wish, though you don't feel over-committed to much right now. Aries now loves to have fun and this week provides that commodity in abundance.

9 WEDNESDAY   *Moon Age Day 11   Moon Sign Aquarius*

Professional matters should go smoothly today, even if in your heart you would rather be somewhere else. It isn't the things you want to do that matter right now but rather the things you have to do. As long as you keep a smile on your face the day should be a breeze.

10 THURSDAY
Moon Age Day 12   Moon Sign Pisces

A slight lack of confidence or commitment typifies what can happen to Aries under the prevailing planetary trends. Don't despair. This time is given to you in order to give you space to get your head together for the very real efforts you will be putting in soon. Take it at face value as a rest from your usually hectic pace.

11 FRIDAY
Moon Age Day 13   Moon Sign Pisces

It is close partnerships that make life most fulfilling now, both in a romantic sense and for those Arians who are in joint professional ventures. Keep a sense of proportion regarding family matters, some of which appear to be giving you a hard time today and tomorrow.

12 SATURDAY
Moon Age Day 14   Moon Sign Pisces

This is an excellent time to broaden your horizons in a general sense but you could also find yourself making specific journeys to interesting places. Certainly, finding yourself stuck in any sort of rut has no appeal whatsoever. Those Arians who can take enjoy an autumn break now are the luckiest of all.

13 SUNDAY
Moon Age Day 15   Moon Sign Aries

Things are heating up and the presence of the lunar high certainly helps you get ahead. You are now dynamic and raring to have a go at things you shied away from only a day or two ago. If you want an October day on which it proves possible to move mountains, this could be it.

14 MONDAY
Moon Age Day 16   Moon Sign Aries

If you are a Monday to Friday worker, the presence of the lunar high at the start of a new working week can only prove to be good news. Good luck is on your side and you can afford to speculate a little, as long as you take care not to overstretch yourself. Social encounters should be positive and offer you new incentives of every sort.

15 TUESDAY — *Moon Age Day 17   Moon Sign Taurus*

You remain in the market for a good time. Sexy and keen to make a good impression, Aries puts on its best display at the moment. Don't be surprised if your flirtatious ways lead to encounters you might not have expected. In moods like this, not everyone you attract may be your intended target.

16 WEDNESDAY — *Moon Age Day 18   Moon Sign Taurus*

There may be conflict at work today and it will be important to take the heat out of situations if at all possible. Although not everyone appears to be your friend at the moment it is difficult to understand why this should be the case. Just be yourself and awkward types should come round in the end.

17 THURSDAY — *Moon Age Day 19   Moon Sign Taurus*

Your love life could take a slightly different direction from the one you had been expecting, possibly because your partner is acting in a somewhat unusual way. This trend need not be at all difficult. On the contrary, it could lead you to an experience or two that might prove to be quite exciting.

18 FRIDAY — *Moon Age Day 20   Moon Sign Gemini*

This would be a lucky day for making decisions of just about any sort. But life is not all about having to make your mind up. On the contrary, you have time on your hands and plenty of opportunity to do something simply because it would be good fun. Your verbal dexterity is likely to come in very handy now, too.

19 SATURDAY — *Moon Age Day 21   Moon Sign Gemini*

You are almost certainly feeling more optimistic now than has been the case for perhaps a couple of weeks. Your cheerful disposition makes you great fun to have around and you won't go short of the right sort of personal attention. Some of the compliments you receive could even be somewhat embarrassing.

20 SUNDAY
Moon Age Day 22   Moon Sign Cancer

Your main focus today is likely to be your domestic life. Not much ruffles your feathers at the moment, though you won't take too kindly to being told what to do. This only really applies if you work on a Sunday. Most home-based situations ought to turn out to be relaxing and peaceful.

21 MONDAY
Moon Age Day 23   Moon Sign Cancer

The intensity of your views, particularly at work, gets you noticed but is it for the right reasons? There are times when you can be a little too outspoken for your own good and it is quite important to allow others to have their say. The failure to do so looks likely to be something of a negative trend during this part of October.

22 TUESDAY
Moon Age Day 24   Moon Sign Leo

Meetings with very interesting people could set this Tuesday apart for you. Many Arians could be taking a well-earned holiday from the practical chores of life, and not simply so that you can take a different set on board instead. Today you need to drop the traces of responsibility and behave like a ten-year-old for a few hours.

23 WEDNESDAY
Moon Age Day 25   Moon Sign Leo

This would be a fine time for practical ideas and for having a generally easy run. Once again it is obvious that how you get the job done is more important than speed and you show some real class when in social situations. It would be hard not to envy Aries when it is in this frame of mind.

24 THURSDAY
Moon Age Day 26   Moon Sign Virgo

Various circumstances should be working in your favour today. This should be a smooth-running period and one during which your natural charm really pays off. Very few people could refuse your seemingly modest requests at the moment and you should find that you have plenty of new friends.

25 FRIDAY
Moon Age Day 27   Moon Sign Virgo

You can get a lot done now as a result of sheer self-discipline, not a quality that Aries universally understands. Once you have made up your mind to a specific course of action, you are unlikely to change it. Routines are now easily dealt with and some of them might even be actively welcomed.

26 SATURDAY
Moon Age Day 28   Moon Sign Libra

A mixture of confusion and not a little incompetence could be the order of the day unless you take some extra care. The Moon isn't going to do you any favours so you really will need to call on the help and support of others in order to get the very best out of today. All in all, it might be best to stay tucked up in bed.

27 SUNDAY
Moon Age Day 0   Moon Sign Libra

Prepare for some hold-ups today as there is little you can do to avoid them. The planets indicate a somewhat careless attitude mixed with a type of lethargy that is far from the usual nature of an Aries so watch out for this and try to curb the instinct if you can. Despite a few negative trends, you should be generally happy this weekend.

28 MONDAY
Moon Age Day 1   Moon Sign Scorpio

There is quite a strong chance that the beginning of this week will coincide with the feeling that your life in general is in a state of some flux. You are better able to deal with such a situation than most zodiac signs would be and you won't worry unduly if you are forced to think on your feet a good deal.

29 TUESDAY
Moon Age Day 2   Moon Sign Scorpio

This is a day during which some organisation and self-discipline could work wonders. It might occur to you that certain elements of your life have been running rather out of control and if this is the case you will want to do something about it as soon as you can. That's fine – but don't go at things like a bull at a gate.

30 WEDNESDAY   *Moon Age Day 3   Moon Sign Sagittarius*

You may be inclined to ignore responsibilities almost totally today, in favour of socializing. There should be little to stop you seeking a good time and there are plenty of people around who will be only too willing to follow your lead. The Moon now helps on the romantic front and love could come knocking.

31 THURSDAY   *Moon Age Day 4   Moon Sign Sagittarius*

You can put your ingenuity to good use today and won't be stuck for a good idea at any stage. Avoid unnecessary routines because these will prove tedious and without any real merit. What you are looking for now is diversity and the chance to manage old jobs in your revolutionary new way.

November 2019

1 FRIDAY
☿ *Moon Age Day 5   Moon Sign Sagittarius*

Today is harmonious in almost every sense. Good contacts with useful people could set the day apart and might find you gaining financially from discussions or transactions. Your enjoyment of life knows no bounds, though you tend to express it in a somewhat low-key fashion while the present planetary picture is maintained.

2 SATURDAY
☿ *Moon Age Day 6   Moon Sign Capricorn*

You may not be thinking very clearly right now and might require the help and support of people who are more in the know than you are. Eating humble pie in order to get the information you need is never a pleasurable experience for Aries but you can content yourself with the knowledge that it is good for your soul.

3 SUNDAY
☿ *Moon Age Day 7   Moon Sign Capricorn*

It may be easy to tell today how many people hold you in high esteem. You could be surprised at the number, particularly since you may learn that you are popular with a few people you didn't think liked you at all. Don't be slow when it comes to asking for what you want, especially in a material sense.

4 MONDAY
☿ *Moon Age Day 8   Moon Sign Aquarius*

You will be at your best if you are required to work as part of a team and at any time when co-operation is necessary. Try to avoid being offhand with people you don't like, as this would be at odds with your generally charming manner today. At work, it is possible that rules and regulations you deem unnecessary will get on your nerves.

5 TUESDAY ☿ *Moon Age Day 9 Moon Sign Aquarius*

This should prove to be the beginning of an industrious period, although consequently you can expect to have less time for enjoyment. Aries is on full alert now and making the most of every opportunity that comes along, but you might want to reflect on how important that is to you if you don't manage to have some fun along the way?

6 WEDNESDAY ☿ *Moon Age Day 10 Moon Sign Pisces*

You are in a forward-looking frame of mind, still anxious to get ahead and only too willing to take a few chances if necessary. Your social relationships should be good but not as positive as your romantic attachments. For at least some Arians this is the romantic high spot of the whole of November.

7 THURSDAY ☿ *Moon Age Day 11 Moon Sign Pisces*

Matters close to your heart are boosted today and your sensitivity is now stronger than ever. Not all your wishes will come true right now but you should be able to put in that extra bit of personal effort that will set many of them on the right path. The world might struggle to keep up with you today.

8 FRIDAY ☿ *Moon Age Day 12 Moon Sign Pisces*

Under changing trends, your powers of influence are a little weaker today so, unusually, you may decide to keep yourself to yourself. Maybe you have already decided on a stay-at-home sort of Friday, and are looking forward to being surrounded by family members and simply putting your feet up.

9 SATURDAY ☿ *Moon Age Day 13 Moon Sign Aries*

Now the Moon races into your zodiac sign, bringing to an end any sticky situations that have prevailed over the last three weeks or so. All is brightness and optimism for Aries now and if you don't realise this, you are not looking hard enough. Treat awkward situations to a dose of good old-fashioned common sense.

10 SUNDAY ☿ *Moon Age Day 14* *Moon Sign Aries*

Waste no time taking a hands-on approach to all vital issues. This might be Sunday, but that doesn't necessarily mean you have to stay clear of practical or professional matters. Although this might not leave much time for leisure pursuits, simply being at the sharp end of things could be fun enough now.

11 MONDAY ☿ *Moon Age Day 15* *Moon Sign Taurus*

There isn't a great deal of logic about today and it appears that at least part of the time you are running on automatic pilot. Although you might find certain people difficult to deal with, you do have great persuasive powers at present and merely have to remind yourself to use them properly.

12 TUESDAY ☿ *Moon Age Day 16* *Moon Sign Taurus*

New avenues of communication tend to open up during this, the most potentially interesting of times. Although it might sometimes be further to the winning post than you might have imagined, it's worth keeping on running in almost any situation. Today can be truly yours with only a modicum of effort.

13 WEDNESDAY ☿ *Moon Age Day 17* *Moon Sign Taurus*

A sort of power struggle seems to be taking place now. If you are not working today this trend is likely to have a bearing on your home life. Although it might seem attractive to be at the head of everything, accept that there are some situations you simply don't understand and which you should leave alone.

14 THURSDAY ☿ *Moon Age Day 18* *Moon Sign Gemini*

Professional objectives may need careful handling at the moment. Your chart indicates some possible defeats in view – and you won't take at all kindly to these. Think before you act and if you are in any doubt, don't act at all. You may have the chance to be involved in social gatherings that could provide a welcome diversion.

15 FRIDAY ☿ *Moon Age Day 19   Moon Sign Gemini*

What happens socially today could help to improve your life in other ways too. The level of confidence you have in yourself is clearly rising but you won't be at peak efficiency for a few days. The actions of family members can give you pause for thought, and perhaps lead to you treating them differently.

16 SATURDAY ☿ *Moon Age Day 20   Moon Sign Cancer*

You make your way in life by having your own ideas and being unafraid of new concepts and the current planetary trends really favour your approach. Aries is extremely innovative at the moment and others would be sensible if they took notice of what you have to say. Friends should be especially attentive towards you.

17 SUNDAY ☿ *Moon Age Day 21   Moon Sign Cancer*

You enjoy travel at the best of times but will take to it extremely well at present. There is something very attractive about simply getting on a train or in the car and setting off. It doesn't matter whether you are travelling for business or fun, it's the getting there that appeals to you during this period.

18 MONDAY ☿ *Moon Age Day 22   Moon Sign Leo*

A charming social performance on your part could impress any number of people. Astrological trends point to a rather unusual sort of start to the week and a time during which you could easily be surprised. Not everyone is going to behave as you might have imagined so you will need some flexibility to cope with the situation.

19 TUESDAY ☿ *Moon Age Day 23   Moon Sign Leo*

Work undertaken in a team and any co-operative ventures may not go as planned now, so if you can try to go it alone. Don't get yourself into a stew about a matter that could be sorted out quite easily. Get cracking early in the day and you should get everything you really want done and out of the way in time to have some leisure hours.

20 WEDNESDAY ☿　　*Moon Age Day 24　Moon Sign Leo*

Although this is hardly the time for grand ideas and flamboyant gestures, there is no reason that today should prove to be particularly difficult. It would be sensible to think of this as a social rather than a practical day. There are influences that will slow situations down somewhat but they won't prevent anything from happening.

21 THURSDAY　　*Moon Age Day 25　Moon Sign Virgo*

All aspects of communication are going extremely well now. With some entertaining people on the horizon and almost everything going your way, the time has come to put your thoughts into tangible form. Almost anyone will be pleased to hear what you have to say and their reactions could be surprising.

22 FRIDAY　　*Moon Age Day 26　Moon Sign Virgo*

You will probably go to great lengths to please others today. There's nothing wrong with this, except for the fact that you may need to prepare to be disappointed with the response. Nevertheless, the self-sacrificing quality you presently show isn't something you can alter. It's simply the way you are at present.

23 SATURDAY　　*Moon Age Day 27　Moon Sign Libra*

If you want a day during which you can make an impact on the world, this is not it. Instead of trying to do everything yourself, allow others to take at least part of the strain. This does not mean you are likely to lose control, so don't get upset about a fairly compulsory layoff that only lasts a day.

24 SUNDAY　　*Moon Age Day 28　Moon Sign Libra*

Sunday should bring a more positive trend, though probably not at first. Be willing to take some time out because this is meant to be a day of rest after all. The chances are that you are well ahead with most tasks and you can afford to relax a little. This is the ideal opportunity to spend more time with your partner.

25 MONDAY *Moon Age Day 29   Moon Sign Scorpio*

Energy is now plentiful and you should have little or no difficulty in getting what you need from life, even if you cannot manage everything you want. Routines are something you wouldn't welcome around now and it is quite obvious that you are up for as much variety as you can get.

26 TUESDAY *Moon Age Day 0   Moon Sign Scorpio*

Your self-determined approach to life seems to be infectious and you will certainly impress both colleagues and strangers at present. You allow nothing to stand in your way but this is not to suggest that you are being ruthless as far as friends are concerned. You will easily find the time to defend and support your pals

27 WEDNESDAY *Moon Age Day 1   Moon Sign Sagittarius*

In group or co-operative matters you make sure you are on the winning side. After a really hectic period you might decide that it's time to simply have some fun and nobody is going to argue with that. Avoid getting involved in a domestic dust-up and show that you are sweetness and light to everyone.

28 THURSDAY *Moon Age Day 2   Moon Sign Sagittarius*

A social or leisure pursuit might take something of a toll on you, which is why you could be slowing things down somewhat today. This seesaw time is nothing particularly unusual for Aries and you cope with it almost without thinking. Respond to the warmth being shown to you by others.

29 FRIDAY *Moon Age Day 3   Moon Sign Capricorn*

It could be that you want to speed things up at work but whether or not others have the same idea will be another matter. The fact is that you may find yourself somewhat hemmed in by red tape around now and will have difficulty proceeding because of it. Turn your mind towards romance, which doesn't have too many restrictions.

30 SATURDAY   *Moon Age Day 4   Moon Sign Capricorn*

Emotional issues could prove to be somewhat demanding at the moment and you might decide to shelve them for a while. It would be best to keep yourself busy in other ways. Certainly there is no shortage of things to be done, either at work or at home and it is possible that you will be quite busy on the social front.

December

2019

1 SUNDAY
Moon Age Day 5   Moon Sign Aquarius

Mental stimulus is what you really need and you will deliberately be offering yourself up for puzzles of one sort or another. These could be practical in nature or simply for the sake of entertainment. There is also much activity today and a desire to get as much preparatory work done as is possible.

2 MONDAY
Moon Age Day 6   Moon Sign Aquarius

With a hectic period commencing both at home and most likely at work, less of your time belongs exclusively to you early this week. However, there is a need to ensure that at least an hour or two out of every day remains available, even if this means you have to put off one or two tasks until after the New Year.

3 TUESDAY
Moon Age Day 7   Moon Sign Aquarius

A change of pace would do you the world of good around now. Leave work issues on the backburner for a couple of days and concentrate instead on what your social life is presently offering. This may not be the best time of all to begin a new health regime but in the end only you can judge.

4 WEDNESDAY
Moon Age Day 8   Moon Sign Pisces

A social contact could develop into something much more if you are an Arian who is open to new romance. Those who are in settled relationships will be consolidating personal attachments and finding moments to say those little words that are most important. Family-motivated interests probably predominate around now.

5 THURSDAY
Moon Age Day 9   Moon Sign Pisces

At this time you possess a charming, understanding and vibrant nature. It would be difficult for anyone to either miss or ignore you, which is great from a social point of view. If there are any last minute arrangements to be made, you could not pick a better day for dealing with them than this one turns out to be.

6 FRIDAY
Moon Age Day 10   Moon Sign Aries

The fact that the lunar high comes along at this time in December could be very telling. You have masses of energy and should be able to operate on several different fronts at the same time. There are significant gains in the offing and a chance to show your mettle at exactly the right time.

7 SATURDAY
Moon Age Day 11   Moon Sign Aries

This is a good time to show everyone exactly what you are made of and to display yourself at your very best ahead of the build up to Christmas. What you say and do today, especially if you are at work, can set the seal on a number of events beyond this year, so it's very important to put in that extra effort.

8 SUNDAY
Moon Age Day 12   Moon Sign Aries

Doing your own thing seems to be the key to happiness at the moment, although it appears possible that your focus is slightly wrong. Join in with some family fun and you will lighten the professional load you could be carrying at present. You may also need to bolster the resolve of a friend who is trying to alter their life. Only you can help with this.

9 MONDAY
Moon Age Day 13   Moon Sign Taurus

This is a good day for getting down to brass tacks at work and for letting others know the way you feel about certain issues. Not everyone will agree with you of course, but when it matters the most you can get people on your side. Don't be surprised if offers of greater responsibility are now coming your way.

10 TUESDAY
Moon Age Day 14   Moon Sign Taurus

Since work matters now seem to be fairly progressive and, in the main, looking after themselves, you will probably be turning your attention to other things. Your confidence remains generally high on the social scene, and you may decide to embark upon new interests that have been at the back of your mind for a while.

11 WEDNESDAY
Moon Age Day 15   Moon Sign Gemini

Today can put you to the test in a number of ways, but probably not more so than at work. You need to show that you are aware of the opposition that is around right now and that you can deal with it easily. Very few people would catch you napping, but it isn't enough to simply recognise this for yourself.

12 THURSDAY
Moon Age Day 16   Moon Sign Gemini

High spirits prevail, and the sense of joy that is so important to your zodiac sign is present. Not everyone is quite as happy as you are today though, but you should be able to cheer anyone up if you put your mind to it. Personal issues demand a matter-of-fact attitude at present.

13 FRIDAY
Moon Age Day 17   Moon Sign Cancer

Being an Arian, it has probably only now finally sunk in that Christmas is just around the corner. You will want to make sure that all details are sorted out as quickly as possible, and with the weekend in view you might already be planning an epic shopping spree. Make all arrangements as much fun as you can.

14 SATURDAY
Moon Age Day 18   Moon Sign Cancer

Along comes a very harmonious period, particularly at home. The weekend is hardly likely to be the most exciting one you have encountered this year, though it does offer a sense of contentment and security that pleases you. Friends may have some unique ideas regarding Christmas.

15 SUNDAY
Moon Age Day 19   Moon Sign Cancer

You should now find it easier to come to terms with slight personal problems. If you take a practical view of most issues you should be able to see through to the heart of any matter and be less inclined to brood and much more likely to take appropriate action. You could end this day feeling that it has been very advantageous all round.

16 MONDAY
Moon Age Day 20   Moon Sign Leo

Happily on the go today, you find the possibility of any sort of travel quite exciting. Whether this means taking some time out for a pre-Christmas break or just braving the crowds to do some necessary Christmas shopping, it's the movement and activity that excites you. A general sense of goodwill seems to pervade your life now.

17 TUESDAY
Moon Age Day 21   Moon Sign Leo

A few small drawbacks at work are possible today, but these might be due to the fact that you find it difficult to keep your mind on the job at hand. In other ways, you are busy right now and possibly getting certain aspects of the festive season slightly out of proportion. Concentrate on the domestic scene.

18 WEDNESDAY
Moon Age Day 22   Moon Sign Virgo

Someone, somewhere, ought to be making you feel really good, simply by saying and doing the right things. You have plenty to occupy your mind right now, but you should spend at least a few moments looking around yourself today and working out where your priorities should be at this time of year.

19 THURSDAY
Moon Age Day 23   Moon Sign Virgo

There is an emphasis today upon pleasure, and finding it wherever you can. Your commitment to the practical side of life is much less emphasised for a day or two, leaving you determined to please yourself in every other way. Bear in mind that not everyone is going to understand your present attitude, though.

20 FRIDAY   *Moon Age Day 24   Moon Sign Libra*

Don't take anything for granted today. This is a time during which you should check and double-check all arrangements. The lunar low might slow you down a little but if you are careful and circumspect it won't prevent you from dealing with your obligations or having some fun.

21 SATURDAY   *Moon Age Day 25   Moon Sign Libra*

While it might be quite difficult to get your own way at present you should still be able to carry on as normal at work. Use your intuition when it comes to assessing others and exert a degree of patience when it comes to getting what you want from practical situations.

22 SUNDAY   *Moon Age Day 26   Moon Sign Scorpio*

A loved one, or your romantic partner, might be expressing some rather strong opinions at present. Be creative in your responses and don't allow yourself to become unsettled by matters that you can deal with quite easily. Trends suggest that even on this Sunday so close to Christmas you may have some interesting opportunities to change aspects of your working life.

23 MONDAY   *Moon Age Day 27   Moon Sign Scorpio*

Today should find you busy and very progressive in attitude. However, the important aspects of today could easily be romantic ones. Maybe it's the time of year or perhaps your own attitude, but you should find that your partner is now very much more responsive and inclined to say just the right things to you.

24 TUESDAY   *Moon Age Day 28   Moon Sign Sagittarius*

Look out for an adaptable attitude and a willingness to learn as you go along. Christmas Eve should prove to be most enjoyable and brings you closer to understanding the true motivations and opinions of family members and friends who have been a closed book to you for some time.

25 WEDNESDAY *Moon Age Day 29   Moon Sign Sagittarius*

It is likely that you will find that what sets this Christmas Day apart is your ability to say exactly what you feel and yet make everyone around you feel very special indeed. Surprises are in store, and although that isn't all that odd on this day some of them will far surpass your expectations and may have nothing to do with gifts.

26 THURSDAY *Moon Age Day 0   Moon Sign Capricorn*

Watch out for strong feelings and a desire for emotional security right now. Make sure this doesn't lead to some unnecessary and potentially destructive jealousy. Everything will turn out just fine if you don't tinker with the nuts and bolts of personal attachments. Simply enjoy what Boxing Day has to offer in an all-round sense.

27 FRIDAY *Moon Age Day 1   Moon Sign Capricorn*

You can accomplish a great deal around now and won't have much difficulty finding people who want to go along with your ideas. Interrupting the flow of festivities, you now have your practical head on and may be turning your thoughts towards work, whether you are actually there or not.

28 SATURDAY *Moon Age Day 2   Moon Sign Capricorn*

Avoid being too extravagant today. There is a possibility that you are spending money you don't actually have, and this could lead to a few worries towards the very end of the year or in January. Be realistic and try to persuade those around you to take a similar attitude.

29 SUNDAY *Moon Age Day 3   Moon Sign Aquarius*

One of your greatest strengths today is your ability to present yourself positively, no matter what company you are in. Arians who are at work today can make the most of plans laid down before Christmas and even if you are not back in harness yet, you should still be able to find some way to get ahead.

30 MONDAY
Moon Age Day 4   Moon Sign Aquarius

You should be in a reflective mood as you look back at the end of one year and towards the beginning of another. You have planned carefully for what lies ahead and so should be feeling quite confident. The deeper thought processes of the Aries mind are definitely brought into play around now.

31 TUESDAY
Moon Age Day 5   Moon Sign Pisces

New Year's Eve brings plenty of good things and you will be on the lookout for new faces and for the sort of people you know are going to be useful to have around in the New Year. Don't be too quick to jump to conclusions in your personal life. It would be far better to ask a few leading questions instead.

RISING SIGNS FOR ARIES

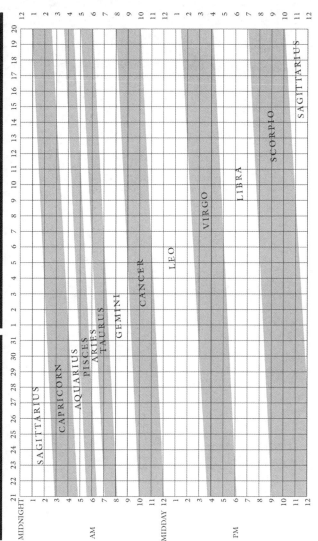

THE ZODIAC, PLANETS
AND CORRESPONDENCES

The Earth revolves around the Sun once every calendar year, so when viewed from Earth the Sun appears in a different part of the sky as the year progresses. In astrology, these parts of the sky are divided into the signs of the zodiac and this means that the signs are organised in a circle. The circle begins with the sign of Aries and ends with Pisces.

Taking the zodiac sign as a starting point, astrologers then work with all the positions of planets, stars and many other factors to calculate horoscopes and birth charts and tell us what the stars have in store for us.

The table below shows the planets and Elements for each of the signs of the zodiac. Each sign belongs to one of the four Elements: Fire, Air, Earth or Water. Fire signs are creative and enthusiastic; Air signs are mentally active and thoughtful; Earth signs are constructive and practical; Water signs are emotional and have strong feelings.

It also shows the metals and gemstones associated with, or corresponding with, each sign. The correspondence is made when a metal or stone possesses properties that are held in common with a particular sign of the zodiac.

Finally, the table shows the opposite of each star sign – this is the opposite sign in the astrological circle.

Placed	Sign	Symbol	Element	Planet	Metal	Stone	Opposite
1	Aries	Ram	Fire	Mars	Iron	Bloodstone	Libra
2	Taurus	Bull	Earth	Venus	Copper	Sapphire	Scorpio
3	Gemini	Twins	Air	Mercury	Mercury	Tiger's Eye	Sagittarius
4	Cancer	Crab	Water	Moon	Silver	Pearl	Capricorn
5	Leo	Lion	Fire	Sun	Gold	Ruby	Aquarius
6	Virgo	Maiden	Earth	Mercury	Mercury	Sardonyx	Pisces
7	Libra	Scales	Air	Venus	Copper	Sapphire	Aries
8	Scorpio	Scorpion	Water	Pluto	Plutonium	Jasper	Taurus
9	Sagittarius	Archer	Fire	Jupiter	Tin	Topaz	Gemini
10	Capricorn	Goat	Earth	Saturn	Lead	Black Onyx	Cancer
11	Aquarius	Waterbearer	Air	Uranus	Uranium	Amethyst	Leo
12	Pisces	Fishes	Water	Neptune	Tin	Moonstone	Virgo